Field Guide to

How to Use and Interpret Charms, Signs, and Superstitions

By Alys R. Yablon

QUIRK BOOKS

PHILADELPHIA

DISCLAIMER
The world of luck is wide and varied. Although we have taken care to
represent widely diverse superstitions, signs, and charms, the author and the
publisher cannot guarantee this guide addresses every possible type worldwide,
nor can they accept responsibility for any bad luck brought on by the
practices described herein.

Copyright © 2008 by Quirk Productions, Inc.

Library of Congress Cataloging in Publication Number: 2007937186

ISBN: 978-1-59474-217-0

Printed in Singapore

Typeset in Adobe Garamond, Franklin Gothic, and Impact

Designed by Karen Onorato
Illustrations by Brian Stauffer
Iconography by Karen Onorato

Distributed in North America by Chronicle Books
680 Second Street
San Francisco, CA 94107

10 9 8 7 6 5 4 3 2

Quirk Books
215 Church Street
Philadelphia, PA 19106
www.quirkbooks.com

Contents

Introduction

Luck is believing you're lucky.—Tennessee Williams

We all do certain things to enhance our fortune. Whether it's wearing a lucky charm, carrying a rabbit's foot, or seeking counsel from a Ouija board, superstitious actions make us feel more in control of our fate and help ease the burden of life's mystery.

In *Field Guide to Luck*, you will encounter more than ninety charms, superstitions, signs, and numbers that are linked to the concept of luck, both good and bad. You will learn what to avoid and what to embrace; how to reverse curses and other runs of bad karma; and how to bring about health, wealth, and happiness. The entries span vast historical, geographical, and cultural chasms. From ancient Egypt, Greece, and China to contemporary America and Africa, and from astrology and numerology to Judaism, Christianity, and Buddhism, the symbols and ceremonies described within will open your eyes to an astonishing array of elaborate practices.

If you have ever wondered why your grandmother was prone to spit midsentence, why your Uncle Marty throws salt over his shoulder, or why Madonna wears a red string tied around her wrist, the answers lie in the pages ahead. Superstitions as common as avoiding black cats and picking up a lucky penny are explained in their historical and cultural contexts, as are less familiar customs, such as worshipping the goddess Lakshmi, donning an evil eye bead, or placing an acorn in your window. In addition to illuminating the historical origins of various actions and objects, the entries discuss how superstitions relate to our lives today. You never know when you might find an opened ladder in your path or a ladybug on your shoulder, so always carry a copy of *Field Guide to Luck*—just in case.

Believing in Superstition

Superstitions are inherently irrational. You cannot scientifically prove that something desirable happened just because you wished for it while watching a shooting star, and there is no way of knowing if garlic truly wards off evil spirits. But two of the most seminal and pervasive forces in our world—namely, love and religion—are similarly irrational. It is impossible to prove the existence of God, just as it is impossible to quantify feelings of love and attraction. Yet religious faith and romantic love are central to so many cultures that they are popularly accepted. Just as we can't explain how a sudden, powerful attraction to a complete stranger can result in the formation of a new family and a relationship that lasts for decades, we cannot always rationalize why we choose to believe in magic, superstitions, or just plain dumb luck.

In the age-old tension between science and religion, superstition has traditionally held a place somewhere in the middle. Medicine men and shamans, sorcerers and witches, priests and Buddhas have all maintained superstitious beliefs and used symbolic objects to heal patients and wound enemies. The Roman Catholic Church has an intimate relationship with all things miraculous, canonizing saints based on their magical healing powers and using ritualized practices, such as rosary beads and prayers, to help alter reality.

We live in a supremely mechanized world, a high-tech, fast-paced environment in which religion is often not the focus. We concentrate on curing illnesses, exploring space, and acquiring the latest technology. For many, formalized religion has taken a backseat to more materialistic pursuits. Yet now more than ever, increasing numbers of people are open to informal faiths that emphasize spiritual experience and psychological awareness. Ancient traditions, from Kabbalah and I Ching to yoga and meditation, are experiencing a revival across religious and geographical lines, gaining popularity as our social consciousness evolves. The New Age movement and its offspring have created an environment in which people can access a wide range of religious expressions.

Perhaps because of this openness, superstition—once regarded as outdated—is back in fashion. The plethora of self-help and self-improvement books only solidifies this trend. We are hungry for something to believe in, something that speaks to us beyond science and religion. We are willing to alter our behavior and take novel, sometimes irrational measures to improve our lives and our world.

How to Get Lucky

If you could be either inherently lucky or hopelessly unlucky, chances are you'd choose the former. Life is filled with ups and downs, and the ups are certainly more fun. So we instinctively look for ways not only to enhance but also to induce those experiences. If you passed a calculus test in high school while wearing your favorite blue T-shirt, you may find yourself donning that top to exams throughout college. Why not? Who's to say it wasn't the comfort and familiarity of the well-worn garment that calmed your nerves and allowed you to focus on the problems you needed to solve to pass the test? And if you once got a flat tire on Friday the thirteenth, and on another such inauspicious date you were fired from your job, you might decide to take that day off in the future, just to be careful.

What many of us would like to know is, How can I be one of the lucky ones? It might be asking a lot to be imbued with the power to pick winning lottery numbers or land a dream job right after graduation, but we all want to get on the right track and enjoy lucky breaks. So how does one achieve good fortune?

Many of the entries that follow will help maximize your chances of getting lucky. They'll explain how to attract business by placing a money cat in your office window or to ensure that your new marriage is financially viable by placing a coin in your shoe on your wedding day. The bottom line is that luck is chiefly a state of mind. If you feel lucky and go about your daily life with a positive attitude, you will be more likely to stumble upon those opportunities that constitute a luck-filled life. If you want to be lucky, you will be lucky, one of these days.

Psychologist Richard Wiseman, author of *The Luck Factor: Changing Your Luck, Changing Your Life*, is convinced that getting lucky is a personal choice dependent upon a set of learned behaviors. Even if you were the kind of kid who got picked last for the kickball team and grew up to be the guy who never had much luck with the ladies, you can change your life by embracing certain essential principles. The main strategies are to maximize your chance opportunities, listen to your instincts, expect good things to happen, and find ways to turn bad luck into good. In other words, if you exude positive energy, you will bring about positive change. If you expect good things to happen (and carry a lucky penny in your back pocket, perhaps), they will. If you make an effort to meet lots of people, some of them are bound to help you achieve your goals. By contrast, if you maintain a negative outlook and never maximize your chances to network, you are sure to bring about an unlucky reality. Luck, therefore, is within your control.

Others disagree. Plenty of bad things happen to good people, and plenty of good things happen to bad people. According to this approach, life happens with or without you. Winning the lottery may be life altering, but mathematically speaking, you did not win—the set of numbers did. You just happened to be holding the ticket. In the realm of statistics, everything is bound to happen at some point, but because we are limited to our personal perspective, we lose sight of that fact and feel special when "lucky" events occur.

Beyond personal attitudes and mathematical probability, you might get lucky through enhanced sensory abilities, such as extrasensory perception (ESP) or psychic powers. If you can predict the future, either through dreams, palm readings, horoscopes, or tarot cards or simply by being attuned to spirits from other dimensions, you can subvert any negative events and find ways to bring about a positive outcome. We may not all be fortune-tellers and palm readers, but we can learn to interpret our astrological signs, the lines on our hands, and the ways in which our personalities do or do not reflect our abilities to get lucky.

Finally, we come to the means of getting lucky most carefully explored in *Field Guide to Luck*, namely, the historical emphases on certain objects, colors, numbers, events, and actions that pervade myriad cultures and endure even in our modern age of reason and science. For something to be considered a lucky charm, it must prove itself in a substantial way. Whether you choose to put your fate in the hands of a voodoo doll, a piece of jade, or a horseshoe hung over your doorway, you will gain something by exploring the history of these widely practiced traditions and popular symbols and by evaluating how they speak to you today.

Good luck!

Field Guide to Luck

ACORN

General Description:

The nut of the oak tree (Quercus *species*). Birds and squirrels, among other animals, feast on these hard fruits and then store the excess in the ground. By hoarding acorns near the trees from which they fell, these creatures help ensure the growth of new oaks. Acorns are said to impart the gifts of wealth, protection of property, and health and are believed to aid in the attraction of the opposite sex.

Origins:

A Norse myth relates how Thor (the god of thunder) was saved from a lightning bolt by taking shelter under a large oak tree. The myth spawned the tradition of putting acorns on one's windowsill to protect a house from lightning (no small threat in times when straw roofs were common).

The English proverb "From little acorns come mighty oaks" suggests that, with patience and persistence, one can accomplish tremendous things. Beyond physical greatness, the acorn-turned-oak symbol represents personal growth and development. Because oaks live so long and grow to such enormous proportions, producing acorns only once they are fully mature, these majestic native North American trees represent endurance and strength. Some Christians liken the germination of the acorn seed and the growth of the new tree to the second coming of Jesus Christ.

In Practice: According to one folkloric tradition, the acorn may be used to determine one's lover or marriage partner. Potential mates each place an acorn in a bowl of water. If the acorns float together, the two should marry. An acorn that sinks is a bad omen, indicating death for the person who placed it in the bowl.

A popular Christmas tree ornament, the acorn often appears as the pull on window blinds, a nod to the Norse myth. Anoint an acorn with oil and carry it in your handbag or pocket to help attract members of the opposite sex. Daubed with three drops of pine oil when the moon is waxing, an acorn buried as closely as possible to the front door of your house will help you gain extra income.

Cultural Context: The Druids believed that carrying an acorn would make one perpetually youthful. This belief has carried through the generations in rural parts of England, where even today some maintain that their youthful spirit is due to the little acorns carried in their pockets. The Greeks also associate the acorn with Artemis, the Greek goddess of fertility. Perhaps this connection relates to other powers that the acorn can impart to its owner, notably the ability to attract members of the opposite sex.

2. 📷   **AKUABA**

General
Description:

In the Akan language of Ghana (in West Africa), akuaba *means "doll."* Hand carved from wood and polished with a dark stain, the akuaba doll stands 8–15 inches (20–40 cm) tall and is characterized by a large, flat, disk-shaped head and a body and arms that form the shape of a cross. The dolls are thought to have special powers as fertility aids, and pregnant women consider them to be talismans for beautiful children. Wealthy women have their dolls adorned with special features such as jewels and flourishes related to their tribe, whereas poor women focus on having delicate features carved into the doll's face.

Origins:

Among the Ashanti (or Asante) people of Ghana, a legend tells of a woman named Akua who commissioned the creation of a wooden doll when she was having difficulty conceiving a child. She bathed and dressed the doll and carried it on her back, just as she would a real baby. Other villagers began mocking her, calling the doll *Akua ba*, "Akua's child." However, Akua soon became pregnant and gave birth to a beautiful daughter. The doll has since been adopted as a symbol of fertility and beauty. Even today, Ghanaian women who wish to become pregnant carry these dolls on their backs in the traditional manner of transporting babies.

Variations: Occasionally the dolls are left at the outskirts of a
town to ward off evil spirits, but their main purpose is
to aid in fertility.

The classic Akuaba doll has a large, oval-shaped
head with flattened facial features and a long, thin
neck covered in rings. Similar dolls made by the Fante
people (located south of the Ashanti) have rectangular
heads, and those from the Bono people (north of the
Ashanti) have triangular heads. The practice, however,
remains the same.

In Practice: African women consider their fertility, and the number of healthy pregnancies and children they produce,
to be essential elements of their social status.
Therefore, they regard Akuaba as serious objects
rather than as playthings. The dolls are consecrated by
priests and treated with special care; each night, they
are washed and put to bed in a ritual manner. They
are also used to teach children, especially girls, about
the responsibilities of motherhood. Once a baby is
born, an Akuaba doll worn during pregnancy is given
to him or her to play with and care for.

Cultural
Context: Not only are Akuaba dolls prevalent among African
women, large quantities are also sold locally as sou-
venirs to tourists; they are available on the Internet as
well. However, a tourist may not always know the
object's cultural significance, and female owners especially should be cautious with displaying the sculpture

if they do not wish to become pregnant (or would prefer an ugly child).

Related
Superstition: Voodoo Dolls

3.   **ALADDIN'S LAMP**

General
Description: *A golden (or brass) oil lamp that, when rubbed by its rightful owner, releases a genie who grants wishes to the owner.* Genies may also reside in a decorative bottle. The lamp (or bottle) may be reproduced on a small scale and worn as a charm.

Origins: This belief originates from the fable "Aladdin and the Wonderful Lamp," one of the many stories in *Arabian Nights* (also known as *The Book of One Thousand and One Nights*). The book is a compilation of epic stories from the Middle East recounted by ill-fated Queen Scheherazade. The queen manages to delay her execution by telling stories to her husband, King Shahryar, every night for 1,001 nights, always ending with a cliffhanger that persuades him to call off her death order night after night, until finally he repeals it altogether.

In this particular story, a poor boy named Aladdin is tricked by a magician posing as his uncle into retrieving a magical lamp from inside a treacherous cave. Once Aladdin realizes that the magician is planning to double cross him, he keeps the lamp for himself and discovers that by rubbing the vessel he summons a genie who offers to grant his wishes. Aladdin uses the lamp to secure riches and fame and to win the hand of the sultan's daughter in marriage.

The name Aladdin comes from the Arabic *Ala'ad-Din*, which translates as "nobility of faith." The word *genie* is related to the pre-Islamic myth of the *jinni* or *djinni*, a type of mystical, ghostlike presence imbued with supernatural powers.

Variations: Some believe that using certain scented oils or candles that emit odors or sensations preferred by the genie will also activate the lamp. In images, the genie is nearly always accompanied by a small wisp of smoke, which perpetuates the belief that burning incense and lighting candles will induce the apparition.

In Practice: Examples of Aladdin's lamp are available for purchase from merchants in Egypt and Arabian countries as well as on the Internet. The belief is that, if you are imbued with pure intentions upon taking possession of this elaborately decorated brass vessel, at the onset of a full moon a genie will rise from within and grant you three wishes per year.

Cultural
Context: This magical lamp evokes the hit Disney movie *Aladdin* (1992), which starred Robin Williams as the voice of the genie, and the American television series

I Dream of Jeannie, which starred Barbara Eden and Larry Hagman and aired from 1965 to 1970. In both, the genie character lives inside a lamp or a bottle (complete with lavish period interiors) and is summoned by the "master."

Christina Aguilera put a metaphorical spin on the legend with her 1999 hit song "Genie in a Bottle," in which she invites the listener to "rub me the right way."

Related Superstitions:

Charm Bracelet, Laughing Buddha

AMBER

General Description:

This deep yellow organic material is made of fossilized resin or sap exuded from prehistoric pine trees. Although not a true mineral, it is often referred to as a gemstone and is prized for its translucence, warm color, and unique surface variations. Authentic amber is about thirty to sixty million years old, and some pieces serve as tiny time capsules of earth's beginnings. As the resin oozed and drizzled down trees, it often trapped debris, such as leaves and insects, within its golden trail. Such prehistoric inclusions add to its value and interest among collectors.

When rubbed with a cloth, amber develops a slight electrical charge and will attract particles such as bits of paper. Found most abundantly in the Baltic region, amber is thought to possess medicinal values, imparting youthfulness and good health.

Origins: Stone Age sun worshippers believed that amber contained the energy of the sun. Ancient Greeks and Romans called it *elektron* ("made by the sun"), because of not only the Stone Age belief but also the resin's electrical properties. The Greeks thought that wearing amber jewelry would herald youthfulness and protect against illness.

In Practice: Amber is used as a semiprecious gemstone in jewelry, for which it may take the form of beads or decorative pendants; it may also be shaped into lucky-symbol charms, such as ladybugs and scarabs. Amber has also been fashioned into mouthpieces for cigars or pipes, presumably because of its ability to prevent the transmission of germs. More decorative than practical, amber nonetheless figures among the amulets many luck enthusiasts would never be without.

Some merchants may try to sell "authentic" amber that is in fact common plastic that has been artificially tinted. To determine if you have the real millennia-old material, place your specimen in a glass of salt water or cola. Plastic will sink to the bottom; true amber will float.

Cultural Context: The *Odyssey*, composed in the eighth or seventh century BCE and attributed to the Greek poet Homer, includes several mentions of amber. It is first com-

pared to the sun and then later appears in the form of
a gold necklace intertwined with amber beads that is
offered to Odysseus's wife, Penelope, to distract her
from a messenger's true task. As Penelope and her
household servants admire the jewelry, deciding on
the best possible price for it, the messenger signals to
one of the women that her getaway ship is ready. She
then takes Odysseus's son Telemachus and slips away
unnoticed.

The resurgence of contemporary interest in amber
may be linked to the 1993 movie *Jurassic Park*, in
which dinosaurs are re-created thanks to DNA found
inside a mosquito trapped in a piece of amber.

Related
Superstitions: Jade, Ladybug, Scarab

APRIL FOOLS' DAY

General
Description: *Also known as All Fools' Day, the first of April is widely
celebrated throughout the Western world as a day of
good-natured trickery and silly hoaxes.* Most people
believe that tricks must be played before noon and
that it's bad luck if you fall for a joke after that time.
April 1 is considered to be a lucky birthday. In astrology, April 1 falls within the "first house," or the first
section of the zodiac wheel that is known as Aries.

Origins:
✝

In 1582 Pope Gregory XIII ordered a new calendar (known today as the Gregorian calendar) to replace the Julian calendar. In the latter, the year began in the spring, around the vernal equinox, and new-year festivities occurred from March 25 (the date of the Feast of Annunciation) through April 1. In the new Gregorian calendar, by contrast, the year begins on January 1. When Charles IX instituted the new calendar in France, news traveled slowly throughout the country. So slowly, in fact, that for several years many French villagers were unaware that the date had changed, and they continued celebrating the new year on April 1. Inevitably, city dwellers heard about these mistimed celebrations and began a tradition of sending their rural compatriots on "fools' errands" and generally mocking them until they accepted the new calendar. Gradually, this tradition spread to England and Scotland and, later, to the British and French colonies in the Americas, where it soon became fully integrated into the cultural fabric.

Variations:
ॐ ✡

Various cultures have similar celebratory days on which people dress in funny costumes, play tricks on one another, and generally have a good time. Citizens of ancient Rome organized the Hilaria festival; adherents of Hinduism enjoy a spring festival known as Holi; and Jewish people celebrate a holiday called Purim. All these events occur near the end of March or the beginning of April, the traditional period of ancient and medieval New Year celebrations.

In Practice: The origins of the trickery associated with April Fools' Day are unknown and still debated; some scholars believe the tradition began in sixteenth-century France. Yet April 1 has long been associated with hoaxes, as recorded in English seventeenth-century sources, notably John Aubrey's *Micellanies* (1696). Specific practices differ by country. In present-day France, the joke is known as a *poisson d'avril* (April fish), and French people pin cut-paper fish on the backs of unsuspecting victims. Why they chose a fish remains a mystery, but the use may relate to the Christian fish symbol known as the ichthys.

The jokes can be elaborate and complex, but most are of the simple, harmless variety: relaying false news, tying a person's shoelaces together, or sending someone on a wild-goose chase or futile errand. Usually, when the dupery has run its course or the person realizes the joke, the trickster cries, "April Fools!"

Cultural Context: Every April Fools' Day, the media improves its ability to deceive trusting audiences. Perhaps the most famous incident occurred in 1957, when the usually staid BBC aired a documentary about spaghetti farmers in Switzerland that appeared on its *Panorama* program. The show included footage of Swiss peasants plucking strands of spaghetti from bushes and carefully laying the pasta in the sun to dry. Gullible viewers phoned in, asking where they could purchase spaghetti bushes. Before announcing that the show was a joke, BBC representatives advised people to place a piece of uncooked spaghetti in a can of tomato sauce and await the miraculous results.

Another well-known hoax took place in 1996, when Taco Bell announced that it had purchased the Liberty Bell, located in Philadelphia, and was planning to rename it the Taco Liberty Bell. The joke unleashed hundreds of phone calls and complaints from outraged Americans.

On April 1, 2007, Google placed an online ad announcing a new way to control the plethora of pesky online files draining users' memory cache. Gmail Paper allowed e-mail users to print, free of charge, "one, one thousand, or one hundred thousand of your emails . . . whatever seems reasonable to you." The no-fee service was made possible by bold ads printed in red on the back of every printed page. Even better, Gmail Paper was free of pop-ups and flash animation. Questions about the environmental viability of the new service? Google assured clients that "Gmail Paper is made out of 96 percent post-consumer organic soybean sputum and thus actually helps the environment. For every Gmail Paper we produce, the environment gets incrementally healthier."

Related Superstitions: Astrological Horoscope, Fish

4. 📷 **ASTROLOGICAL HOROSCOPE**

General
Description:
Ω

Astrology is the study of how the sun, moon, and planets—along with their positions relative to one another—influence earthly events. An imaginary band of sky that follows the sun's annual trip around the earth, the zodiac is divided into twelve parts represented by individual signs. Each sign corresponds to specific dates (see chart on page 21). People have long studied the zodiac to understand their place in the world, interpret events, and predict the future. Horoscopes, the forecasts of events based on astrology, are consulted to determine one's luck or fate under various circumstances.

Origins:

The use of the astrological horoscope to study human behavior and analyze events dates back to ancient Mesopotamia, more than five thousand years ago. The word *astrology* derives from the Greek word *astrologia*, meaning "star study"; *horoscope* comes from the Greek *horoskopos*, or "hour watcher."

In Practice:

In Western astrology, the signs of the Zodiac are related to—and named for—constellations. Each sign has its own symbol and "house," or position in the universe. To determine your sign, use the chart on page 21 to find the group your birth date falls into.

Zodiac signs are categorized not only by date but also by energy, planet, and elements. These symbolic associations are used to determine the compatibility of love relationships and the correspondence of events to the alignment of the planets; they may also be consulted to aid in making all types of life decisions, from the trivial to the monumental. Of the four basic elements, fire (Aries, Leo, and Sagittarius) represents energy; earth (Taurus, Virgo, and Capricorn) indicates practicality; air (Gemini, Libra, and Aquarius) symbolizes the intellect; and water (Cancer, Scorpio, and Pisces) denotes emotion. The two basic energies of the universe are yin and yang. Yin (the feminine, receptive energy) includes Taurus, Cancer, Virgo, Scorpio, Capricorn, and Pisces; yang (the male, directive energy) includes Aries, Gemini, Leo, Libra, Sagittarius, and Aquarius.

As in Chinese astrology (see page 49), Zodiac signs embody certain personality traits, as described opposite.

- Like the ram with which they are associated, those born under the sign of **Aries** are strong, assertive, and fiercely loyal. Their somewhat aggressive nature can get them into trouble, especially when arrogance takes control. But their dynamic personality makes them good leaders, though it's best to hold their rash tendencies in check. Compatible with Aquarius, Gemini, Leo, Libra, Sagittarius.

- A typically stubborn **Taurus** will persevere to the bitter end. Yet despite a somewhat bullish side, those

House	Sign	Symbol	Dates
1	Aries	Ram	21 Mar–19 Apr
2	Taurus	Bull	20 Apr–20 May
3	Gemini	Twins	21 May–21 Jun
4	Cancer	Crab	22 Jun–22 Jul
5	Leo	Lion	23 Jul–22 Aug
6	Virgo	Virgin	23 Aug–22 Sep
7	Libra	Scale	23 Sep–22 Oct
8	Scorpio	Scorpion	23 Oct–21 Nov
9	Sagittarius	Archer	22 Nov–21 Dec
10	Capricorn	Goat	22 Dec–19 Jan
11	Aquarius	Water Bearer	20 Jan–18 Feb
12	Pisces	Fish	19 Feb–20 Mar

born under this sign also possess notable artistic qualities and an indulgent, sensual propensity that nicely complement their dependable, resourceful nature. They impart a cozy feeling to others. Compatible with Cancer, Capricorn, Pisces, Scorpio, Virgo.

• Forming one half of a pair of twins, the **Gemini** is naturally communicative and gregarious. At home in most group situations, this social butterfly tends to be a bit gossipy and somewhat cunning. But an inquisitive mind makes Gemini an interesting partner. Compatible with Aries, Aquarius, Leo, Libra, Sagittarius.

- Calling a **Cancer** a crab is a bit of a misnomer. Those born under this sign are tenacious, it's true, but they are also sensitive, protective, and sympathetic. Cancer's maternal or familiar instincts and flair for problem solving result in a caring, reliable partner. Compatible with Capricorn, Pisces, Scorpio, Taurus, Virgo.

- Proud **Leo** is dramatic and dignified. A passionate risk-taker, Leo must mitigate a tendency to be boastful, stubborn, and egotistical to avoid alienating others. Endowed with a bright disposition, generous attitude, and affectionate nature, Leos attract many admirers. Compatible with Aquarius, Aries, Gemini, Libra, Sagittarius.

- **Virgo** shares subtle qualities with the sign's symbol, a virgin, including a tendency toward shyness and modesty. But Virgo's true nature is analytical, efficient, and industrious. An idealistic attitude may, after suffering many disappointments, become cynical and hard. Compatible with Cancer, Capricorn, Pisces, Scorpio, Taurus.

- Always in search of balance, diplomatic **Libra** lives up to the sign's symbol of scales. Endowed with artistic abilities, Libra exhibits a penchant for wit and charm. Sometimes lazy, Libra may appear indecisive. Compatible with Aquarius, Aries, Gemini, Leo, Sagittarius.

- Beware the scorpion's sting. **Scorpios** are a prickly lot, but sometimes a fiery spirit is needed to combat obstacles and solve problems. A keen sense of perception and penetrating intensity lend Scorpios an air of mystery; they are prone to fits of jealousy as well. Many are attracted to their magnetic personality and passionate sexuality. Compatible with Cancer, Capricorn, Pisces, Taurus, Virgo.

- Those born under the sign of **Sagittarius** tend to be fun-loving and extroverted. This optimistic charmer with an adventurous spirit is welcome in any group setting. Frank to the point of brutal honesty, Sagittarius can seem cruel but means no harm. Compatible with Aries, Aquarius, Gemini, Leo, Libra.

- Graced with a sure-footed determination characteristic of its symbol, the goat, friendly **Capricorn** is prudent, hard working, and goal oriented. Such qualities come with a price, however, and Capricorn's dogged spirit may result in obstinacy. Capricorn's good nature is sometimes overshadowed by a tendency to hold grudges. Compatible with Cancer, Pisces, Scorpio, Taurus, Virgo.

- Inventive and unorthodox, **Aquarius** goes with the flow, like the water pouring from the sign's emblem. A humanitarian at heart, generous Aquarius seeks the highest principles in humanity. This tendency toward elitism can lead to conflict, against which Aquarius rebels with ferocity. Compatible with Aries, Gemini, Leo, Libra, Sagittarius.

- Like the dual fish of the sign's symbol, **Pisces** often face two choices and must choose one direction. Sensitive and emotional, those born under this sign nevertheless exhibit surprising fortitude and strength. Their empathy further strengthens their appeal. Compatible with Cancer, Capricorn, Scorpio, Taurus, Virgo.

Horoscopes are published regularly—daily, weekly, monthly—in newspapers and magazines and on Web sites. Based on your sign, find your personal horoscope in a variety of published sources and consult them regularly or as needed. You may also visit an astrologer, who will create a chart that maps the precise alignment of relevant stars and planets at the moment of your birth. Many people use such charts to guide them through myriad decisions, from simple daily activities to major life choices.

Cultural Context:

In 1969 the Fifth Dimension released a hit song called "Aquarius/Let the Sunshine In," popularly known as "The Age of Aquarius." It appeared in the second act of the 1960s musical *Hair* and later formed part of the soundtrack for the 1994 movie *Forrest Gump*. The song refers to the belief that each zodiac sign corresponds to a particular age; the Age of Aquarius was believed to begin at the end of the twentieth century. Following the Age of Pisces, which was dominated by war and suffering, the Age of Aquarius was believed to be filled with love, enlightenment, and other peaceful sentiments popular in the 1960s.

Related
Superstitions:

April Fools' Day, Birth Number, Chinese Astrology, Destiny Number, Fortune Tellers, Master Numbers, Vedic Astrology

BEGINNER'S LUCK

General
Description:
☺

A phenomenon that occurs when someone who is new to a particular game or skill manages to out-play or succeed beyond more experienced individuals. Often used in gambling and sports contexts.

Origins:

Although the exact origin is unknown, the idiom "beginner's luck" became part of North American lingo about the end of the nineteenth century and into the early twentieth.

Variations:

The Rosenthal effect (also known as the teacher-expectancy effect) suggests that students who are expected to perform at a high level are more likely to do so than those lacking similar encouragement. Beginner's luck conflicts with this theory, illustrating instead that someone with no performance expectations—one who may in fact possess absolutely no skill for the task at hand—may be more likely to succeed because he or she is relieved of the pressure of knowing all the details and rules. The complexity of knowledge sometimes hinders success, and ignorance may indeed be bliss.

In Practice: A perfect way to test beginner's luck is to play a game of pool with your friends (or join a group of strangers engaged in play). This scenario assumes that (1) you have never played billiards; (2) you have no idea whether or not you will be good at it; and (3) one or more of the other players have some experience with the game. If within moments you figure out how to hold the stick properly and shoot every striped ball into a pocket, then you will have been graced with beginner's luck. Your adversaries, however, may be less amused at the results of this experiment, especially if placing a bet was part of the game.

Cultural   In November 2006, the London *Times* reported a
Context: story about Carl Smith, who was fishing with friends in the Ebo River in Spain when he caught the biggest catfish ever recorded in the sport of European angling. The fish weighed 226 pounds (103 kg), measured 8 feet long (2.4 m), and took 35 minutes to reel in. The most surprising fact: It was Smith's first time fishing.

Related   Lady Luck
Superstitions:

BIRTH NUMBER

Other Name: Life path.

General   *A birth number is a major component of numerology, an*
Description: *occult science that purports the existence of mystical rela-*
                   tionships between numbers and objects or people. A per-
                   son's birth number is computed by converting the
                   numerals of the birth date into a single number
                   between 1 and 9. This number represents major per-
                   sonality traits, both positive and negative (see "In
                   Practice," page 28).

Origins: Numerology dates back at least to antiquity, when it
                   was favored by ancient Greek mathematicians, includ-
                   ing Pythagoras (569–470 BCE). Other roots include
                   Kabbalah, the ancient Jewish mystical tradition.
                   Numerologists seek correlations between a person's
                   significant numbers and the planets to which those
                   numbers correspond. Each planet assigned a
                   numerical value and is imbued with characteristics
                   (Venus, for example, is the planet of love). Therefore,
                   a birth number greatly influences the foundation of a
                   person's personality and character traits. Once a birth
                   number has been determined, numerologists use the

information to help guide important life decisions, such as when to marry, change jobs, move to a new city, and the like.

In Practice: There are nine birth numbers, or life paths, and each has a set of distinct character traits, similar to the twelve signs of the zodiac. They are:

Birth Number	Character Trait	Planet	Astrological Sign
1	Originator	Sun	Leo
2	Peacemaker	Moon	Cancer
3	Life of the Party	Jupiter	Sagittarius
4	Conservative	Uranus	Aquarius
5	Nonconformist	Mercury	Gemini & Virgo
6	Romantic	Venus	Taurus & Libra
7	Intellectual	Neptune	Pisces
8	Big Shot	Saturn	Capricorn
9	Performer	Mars	Aries

For example, to determine the birth number for April 18, 1976, first add the digits of the month, day, and year (4 + 18 + 1976 = 1998). Then add the digits of that sum (1 + 9 + 9 + 8 = 27) and continue adding the digits of that sum (2 + 7 = 9) until the result falls between 1 and 9. In this case, the birth number is 9.

Cultural Context:

Don Imus, a controversial radio talk-show host, was ousted from the airwaves in 2007 after making offensive, racist comments about members of the Rutgers University women's basketball team. Throughout his long career (he hosted the popular *Imus in the Morning* show from 1971 to 2007), Imus became famous for his shocking humor and on-air pranks. Numerologists were probably the least surprised to learn that he lost his job as a result of the incident. Imus was born on July 23, 1940, making his birth number an 8, which corresponds to the "Big Shot" set of character traits. Eights are known to be misunderstood, arrogant, cold, blunt, and serious about their need to be in charge.

Related Superstitions:

Astrological Horoscope, Destiny Number, Master Numbers, Vedic Astrology

5.   **BLACK CAT**

General Description:
☺☹

A type of small, carnivorous animal (Felis catus) *of any breed whose coat is entirely black.* Cats were domesticated by humans between four and eight thousand years ago and are popular pets worldwide. Equipped with superior predatory skills, retractable claws, and keen sense of sight, hearing, and smell, cats are prized for their ability to hunt small rodents. Also noteworthy are their muscular, compact bodies. Depending on the culture, a black cat is regarded as a harbinger of either good or bad luck.

Origins: Cats were worshipped by ancient Egyptians, who often embalmed, mummified, and buried their felines as elaborately as they did their deceased family members and pharaohs. Black cats began to be interpreted as bad-luck symbols during medieval times, when they became associated with witchcraft and Satan; they were believed to be the animal spirits of witches and often burned alive. Early Christians believed that a black cat crossing your path intended to block your entrance to heaven, and therefore they needed to be destroyed. Today in the United States and many European countries, this occurrence still portends bad luck. The opposite is true in Japan, Ireland, and Britain, where a black cat signifies good things to come.

Variations: In Italy, a black cat sleeping on the bed of a sick person means that the person will soon die. In England, black cats are thought to prevent danger, particularly perils at sea, so fishermen's wives often keep one at home to safeguard their husbands. In Scotland a black cat crossing a porch is a sign of coming wealth.

In Practice: Several cultures propose different solutions to counteract the bad luck bestowed upon you when a black cat crosses your path. In Russia, the popular response is to continue on your way while holding a button for protection. People in other parts of the world believe that you should take twelve steps backward to reverse the bad luck. Still others advise petting the cat three times while speaking in a soothing tone.

Cultural Context:

Because of the association with witches, black cats are especially popular on Halloween. The image of a black cat, with back arched and fur standing on end and with claws and teeth bared, is found carved into pumpkins and engraved on "Happy Halloween" banners worldwide.

The popular television series *Sabrina the Teenage Witch* (1996–2003) featured an adolescent witch-in-training receiving pointers and life lessons from her two aunts, Hilda and Zelda (both witches). Providing much comic relief and a unique brand of counsel was the family's black cat, Salem, a warlock who had been turned into a cat as punishment for attempting world domination (thus explaining how the cat can speak).

Related Superstitions:

Maneki Neko, Nine Lives of Cats

BLUE

General Description:

A color that forms part of the visible spectrum, lying between green and violet, and considered to be one of the three primary colors, along with red and yellow. Because the human eye perceives such natural phenomena as the sky and the sea to be blue, cultures throughout the ages have associated the hue with all things divine.

Origins:

Blue is considered to be a lucky color, notably in the Jewish tradition. In societies worldwide, particularly Middle Eastern cultures, blue is is endowed with the special power to help ward off the evil eye.

In Practice:

In Judaism, blue claims special standing among colors. In the Bible, the description of the *tzitzit*, a four-cornered garment (related to the better-known *tallit*, or prayer shawl) worn by men to remind them of their connection to God, is the command: "Let them attach a cord of blue to each corner" (Numbers 15:38). This blue string was originally made from a dye found in a Mediterranean fish, and it was meant to remind people that ultimately everything comes from God. In many synagogues, particularly those in Sephardic (North African) communities, walls and ornamentation are painted sky blue. The color appears throughout Kabbalistic texts and in jewelry worn by both Jewish and Muslim traditionalists, particularly in such charms as the hamsa or evil eye bead.

Cultural Context:

The design of the Israeli flag shows a modern manifestation of the biblical commandment to weave blue strands into a prayer shawl. Set against a white background is a blue Star of David, with a horizontal blue stripe above and below. White is symbolic of faith, and blue of Godliness. The stripes recall those used to decorate the *tallit*, and the Star of David represents triumph. Together, they form a powerful symbol evoking perseverance and accomplishment.

Related Superstitions:

Evil Eye; Hamsa; Nazar Boncugu; Something Old, Something New, Something Borrowed, Something Blue

---

6. "BREAD AND BUTTER"

General Description:

A phrase spoken to attract protection when two people who are closely related or in a friendship or love relationship are separated by an obstacle while walking together. Saying "bread and butter" ensures that they will not be separated later in a more substantial way.

Origins:

Although the origins of this superstitious incantation are undocumented, it is quintessentially American. It was first recorded as a tradition among schoolchildren in Kansas as early as 1939. The *Dictionary of American Regional English* traces it to the publication that year of the Federal Writers Project's "Guide to Kansas."

In Practice:

It is bad luck for two people to walk on opposite sides of an obstacle, such as a phone booth, a fire hydrant, or an approaching person. To reverse the ill fortune, both parties should say either "Bread and butter!" or "Bread and butter, stick together!" or, even, "Peanut butter and jelly!" The invocation is meant to evoke a sense of togetherness, "sticking" you and your partner back together as though the obstacle had never come between you. To guarantee even greater safety, clasp the other person's hand while uttering the phrase, making it a more physical expression.

Cultural Context:

In the 1939 Warner Brothers/Merry Melodies animated short "A Day at the Zoo," director Tex Avery creates a parody of newsreels from that era. The zoo depicted in the movie includes an American greyhound (a bus driving its way through the zoo), a pack of camels (smoking cigarettes), rabbits multiplying (on adding machines), a jail bird in striped pajamas and chains, a stool pigeon seated on (you guessed it) a stool, and an elephant whose luggage trunk has not yet arrived from Africa. Among these animals are two lions separated by a central pole and pacing in their cage. The lions pace back and forth, back and forth, repeating to one another, "Bread and butter, bread and butter."

Related Superstitions:

"Break a Leg," "God Bless You," "Third Time's a Charm"

"BREAK A LEG"

General
Description:
☺

A phrase spoken, usually with great enthusiasm, to a person about to perform on stage. Saying "Break a leg!" is supposed to bring good luck to the performer by tricking evil spirits, whose attention would otherwise be drawn by the much more obvious "Good luck."

Origins:

Numerous theories exist to explain the origins of this phrase. In ancient Greece, at the end of a performance the audience would stomp their feet rather than clap. In that context, the phrase may have referred to putting on such a good performance that the ensuing enthusiastic stomping would cause audience members to break their legs. In Shakespearian England, the audience would "tip" the actors by throwing money on stage, causing the cast to "break their legs" bending to pick up the coins. (Incidentally, this tradition is thought to have led to the modern custom of throwing flowers on stage in appreciation of a good performance.) More generally, the phrase is a wish for the actor's performance to be so successful that the audience demands a leg-breaking abundance of bows or curtsies at curtain call. A likelier explanation is that, because the curtains at the sides of a stage are called legs, to "break a leg" meant that the actor would need to pass through several times during an encore or curtain call, thus weakening the curtains.

Some people theorize that the "break a leg" phrase dates to 1865, the year that John Wilkes Booth jumped onto the stage of Ford's Theatre after having assassinated President Abraham Lincoln. In the process, he broke his leg. Though Booth was an actor and the incident did take place in a theater, it would be hard to argue that this historical moment was a harbinger of good luck for future actors.

Variations: Other theater superstitions include never whistling in a theater or a dressing room, never uttering the final line of a play during the dress rehearsal, and, most important, never referring to Macbeth in or around a theater. This last tradition, implying that Shakespeare's masterpiece is inherently unlucky to actors and their plays, dates back as far as its first production in the early 1600s. Legend says that the actor playing the role of Lady Macbeth suddenly became ill just before the debut and that Shakespeare himself had to fill in. King James, for whom the play had been written, was so unimpressed with the production that he banned it for five years. In the 1700s, a Dutch actor playing the role of Macbeth killed the actor playing Duncan, stabbing him with a real dagger before a horror-stricken audience. In the 1840s, dozens of people were trampled to death at a performance of the play in New York. Over the years, many actors and audience members have died, experienced grave accidents, narrowly escaped unfortunate prop disasters, or fallen victim to burns, robberies, and muggings. So serious is this superstition among actors that even saying the word "Macbeth" causes people to run out of a theater, spin around several times while shouting profanities, and then beg forgiveness of the Bard himself before daring to re-enter the building. One explanation for the play's disastrous theatrical history is that when it was first published, witches and those believing in the supernatural took offense at the characters of the three witches and placed an irreversible curse on the play.

In Practice: On the opening night of a play, actors warm up their voices and roll back their shoulders in preparation for their debut performances. As the house lights dim and the audience falls quiet, the first actor to appear on stage takes one last, deep breath. Before walking out to deliver the opening lines, he is patted on the back by fellow actors, who wish their colleague the best by whispering, "Break a leg!"

Cultural Context: In the Mel Brooks movie and Broadway musical *The Producers*, corrupt producer Max Bialystock and his milquetoast accountant Leo Bloom plot to produce the worst play ever, *Springtime for Hitler*, hoping that it will be so offensive that it will close on opening night, allowing them to make a fortune on the money they have collected from private donors (unsuspecting old ladies who are in love with Max). On opening night, they are confident that the play will bomb, and in the number "It's Bad Luck to Say Good Luck on Op'ning Night," the pair insist on saying "Good luck" again and again, despite the actors' begging to be told "Break a leg" instead. Unfortunately, their plan backfires, and the play is an unexpected success, landing Bialystock and Bloom in big trouble.

Related
Superstitions:

"Bread and Butter," "God Bless You," "Third Time's a Charm"

7.   **BROKEN MIRROR**

General
Description:

The purposeful or inadvertent shattering of any type of mirrored surface, by dropping, hitting, high-pitched singing, or shocking reflection. Performing such an act is said to bring seven years' worth of bad luck. When an undisturbed mirror spontaneously falls off a wall and shatters upon hitting the floor, it is a sign that someone in the house is at risk of death.

Origins:

Since their invention in antiquity, mirrors are believed by many to possess magical powers—specifically, the power to hold a human soul. Therefore, when a mirror is broken, the body and soul of its owner are also damaged. Seven years are needed to heal. Because mirrors (and other reflective surfaces, such as water) were thought to have fortune-telling powers as well, breaking one forebodes an unpromising future.

Variations: In many cultures worldwide, mirrors are covered in homes where people are in mourning. Doing so is believed to aid the soul of the recently deceased in its journey to the afterlife. If the mirror were revealed, the soul could become trapped within, or—worse—the dead soul might lure a living soul into the afterworld, via the living person's reflection. Vampires, those notoriously soulless creatures, cast no reflection in mirrors.

In Practice: The unlucky victim of a broken mirror can take several actions to counteract the harsh seven-year sentence brought on by the unfortunate mishap. Most popular is waiting seven hours from the time of the breakage (one hour for each year), gathering the shards, and then burying them outside under the light of the moon. Another tactic is to grind the shards into a fine dust, for where there are no shattered reflections, there can be no shattered luck. Yet another practice is to turn counterclockwise three times in front of the broken pieces and then take one shard to a graveyard and touch it to a gravestone. Enslaved Africans developed their own unique practice: They released the shards into a stream, believing that the flow of water would wash away the bad luck.

Cultural Context: In Alfred Hitchcock's classic 1956 film *The Wrong Man*, Henry Fonda plays Manny Balestrero, a working-class man who is incarcerated after being wrongly accused of a crime. As a result of the gross injustice, his wife, Rose, becomes increasingly insane. In one of the more poignant scenes of her character's unraveling, Rose sees Manny's face reflected in a broken mirror, and the distortion causes her to slip into madness. Seeing her husband's altered and unfamiliar reflection, Rose assumes the guilt that her husband does not experience, allowing him to maintain the peace of mind of an innocent person.

8.   **CARRYING A BRIDE OVER A THRESHOLD**

General
Description:
☺

Among newly married couples, the practice of the groom lifting the bride in his arms and carrying her over the threshold of the home they will share together.

Origins:

The original act of carrying the bride over the threshold may have been performed more out of necessity than for purely symbolic reasons. In ancient times as well as in certain present-day patriarchal or agricultural societies, women are sometimes kidnapped and forced to marry, thus necessitating the act of carrying the unwilling particpant to ensure her compliance. Out of this practice developed the tradition of carrying the bride both to demonstrate that she was somewhat reluctant to give up her prized virginity and to make a public statement that she was going to be "taken" by her new husband.

Yet another theory relates to evil spirits that could lurk inside a newly married couple's home. To prevent the malevolent specters from entering through the bride's feet, she had to be carried over the threshold. On a more practical level, carrying the bride ensures that she will not trip upon entering her new home (an action believed to bring bad luck to the couple). Yet another, more obscure reason to lift the bride over the threshold is that the groom's family may have brushed the doorframe with honey, symbolizing the start of the "honeymoon" and the commencement of the couple's sweet life together; by lifting her up, her groom ensures that her wedding gown will not be ruined by the sticky coating.

In Practice: Nowadays, most brides are carried over the threshold of the hotel room where they will be spending their honeymoon. By the time the couple returns to their new abode, the excitement of the moment may have passed and they may neglect to perform the tradition at the appropriate time.

Cultural Context: In an article titled "Why Fat Jokes Aren't Funny" (*USA Today*, posted 6 June 2006), an accountant named Barbara D'Souza describes the conundrum encountered when she and her new husband arrived home after their wedding. D'Souza explains that she is morbidly obese, making it nearly impossible for her to be picked up and carried over the threshold.

Confronted with this "unexpected obstacle," she quickly devised a solution: She gathered up her husband and carried *him* over the threshold instead. Through the example of this simple wedding tradition and the unexpected turmoil it caused her, D'Souza highlights just one of the myriad, often hidden problems faced by overweight people. Her story concludes with the following hope: "Perhaps, in time, we will be able to find social solutions [to the problems caused by being overweight] as carefree as when—instead of crying at our threshold—I merely laughed with my husband and picked him up, happy that I could squeeze him through the doorway."

Related
Superstitions:

Grooms Seeing Brides; Something Old, Something New, Something Borrowed, Something Blue

9.

CHAI

General
Description:

🙂

A symbol composed of heth *and* yod*, two letters from the Hebrew alphabet.* The Hebrew word *chai* means "living" and is traditionally equated with the number 18 (see "Origins"), which is considered to be lucky. It is related to the Hebrew word for "life," *chaim,* and thus to the popular toast *l'chaim,* "to life," spoken in the hopes of engendering good luck and good fortune.

| Origins: | In the Jewish tradition, the practice of gematria assigns a numerical value to each letter. Much has been made of this mystical science, which is used for such varied purposes as deciphering biblical codes and predicting the future. According to gematria, the two letters that spell *chai*—*heth*, which equals 8, and *yod*, which equals 10—add up to 18. The good associations of the word have thus become linked to its numerical equivalent. |

| In Practice: | The word *chai* most commonly appears in jewelry; it is worn as a good luck charm on necklaces and bracelets to affirm life and health. Donations to synagogues and other Jewish charities are often given in increments of eighteen. Chai ($18) or double chai ($36), and variations thereof ($180 and $360), are popular wedding and bar mitzvah gifts. |

| Cultural Context: | Closely derived names are Chaim (for men) and Chaya (for women). One Jewish tradition states that if a baby becomes sick or must undergo surgery, his or her name is changed to Chaim or Chaya to trick the Angel of Death and help ensure a speedy recovery and subsequent good health. |

| Related Superstitions: | Charm Bracelet, Lucky Number 7, Unlucky Number 13 |

CHAIN LETTER

General
Description:

A letter sent by post or e-mail that attempts to lure the recipient into forwarding a copy of the missive to a specified number of people. Part of the instruction often includes sending a sum of money with the letter. The contents of chain letters usually include various emotionally manipulative means to prompt the recipient into action, such as the aim of helping others, receiving great fortunes, and avoiding calamity. Those who continue the chain are promised good luck, money, happiness, political change, or another desired outcome. Recipients are warned of bad luck or financial loss if they "break" the chain by refusing to participate. The advent of online mass mailing lists has enabled the chain-letter fad to spread to every imaginable topic, from politics to recipe exchanges to get-rich-quick pyramid schemes.

Origins:

Historian Daniel VanArsdale notes that chain letters circulated in Europe as early as the eighteenth century. They included apocryphal missives claiming to have divine origins, indicating that they may have stemmed from the Roman Catholic tradition of circulating prayers in church. According to VanArsdale, the first known chain letter dates to about 1888. In it, people were instructed to send dimes to support the education of "poor whites in the region of the Cumberlands." In return, they were promised God's blessing.

Variations:　　The modern-day e-mail chain arrives in many guises. Some of the more popular forms are requests for charity, calls to political action, or invitations to participate in communal friendship-related activities (for example, recipe sharing or a survey or personality questionnaire). Just a few examples of the types of chain letters that may one day appear on your screen or pass through your hands include the following: a petition to sign and then send to others in support of a political or popular cause; a group of funny or inexplicable photographs; a list of jokes; a final-wish plea from a dying child to send the letter to a million people; a feel-good story (often written in iambic pentameter); or a computer-virus warning that may or may not be a hoax.

Perhaps two of the most infamous chain letters in recent history involved the divulgence of "secret" cookie recipes. They began circulating in the late 1980s and purported to reveal how to make the much-loved chocolate chip cookies served by Neiman Marcus and Mrs. Field's, respectively. The letters were supposedly sent in retaliation for bad customer service received at the popular chains. Several versions of these related urban legends exist, most claiming that a woman requesting the recipe was charged an exorbitant fee for the information. She then retaliated by sending the recipe to all her friends, urging them to pass it along to ten of their friends, and so on, in the hopes of putting the offending chain out of business. It didn't work, although each company did receive its share of irate sympathetic complaints in defense of the poor woman.

In Practice: If you receive a chain letter or e-mail, you can expect several things. First, at the bottom of the letter you will notice a list of names of people you may or may not know. You are instructed to send money, wishes, or your signature to the first person on the list, add your name to the bottom of the list, and make a certain number of copies to forward to the people on the list. Then you wait for something good to happen. More often than not, you have just wasted time and money, and you may have even committed a crime (see "Cultural Context," below). If you ignore the letter's directives, you break the chain and take your chances with bad karma.

Cultural Context: Chain letters requesting that you send money or personal possessions are considered unofficial lotteries. According to federal law, they are illegal in the United States. Most other types of chain letters, although they commit the offense of clogging up your inbox or mailbox, are harmless and, with luck, may bring you some joy and laughter.

Related Superstitions: Karma

10. 📷 **CHARM BRACELET**

General
Description:
🙂

A simple chain-link bracelet designed so that one can attach varied charms to the links. The wearer thus benefits from several lucky symbols at once.

Origins:

Charm bracelets date to antiquity. Ancient Egyptians created and used symbolic amulets that described facts about their lives—their home, profession, family members, and so on—to help the gods direct them to the proper place in the afterlife. Charms were also used to ward off evil spirits or to please the gods. During the medieval period in Europe, knights identified themselves by wearing charms indicating their family seal or rank; Jews and Christians wore special charms to confirm their religious identifications. In nineteenth-century England, Queen Victoria brought charm bracelets back into fashion. In America during the postwar era and the early 1950s, young girls and women began in earnest to gather charm collections when their fathers and husbands brought home trinkets from the European and Pacific locales where they had been stationed during the war. Charm bracelets soon became all the rage, and their popularity continues today.

Variations:

One popular charm is the "best friends" heart—a whole charm separated in the middle to appear broken into two pieces. Each friend wears one half as a reminder that something is always missing when the other friend is absent.

In Practice: There are endless charms to collect, from good-luck amulets such as ladybugs and arrowheads to religious symbols to everyday items like shoes, sailboats, and teacups. Collectors scour the earth for the most interesting examples. A common practice is to collect mini-landmarks, such as the Eiffel Tower, Big Ben, or Empire State Building. An alternative—and one that can add a fun mission to your travels—is to collect charms that remind you of a specific place: In China pick up a piece of carved jade, in England a British flag, in Canada a maple leaf, and so on. One by one, the charms are added until the bracelet becomes a unique memento of personal experiences.

Cultural Context: When French luxury fashion house Louis Vuitton released a collection of high-end charms in 2006, style mavens worldwide clamored for the tiny trinkets. The Extraordinary Charms line includes a plethora of adorable baubles sold separately or strung on stunning yellow or white gold bracelets and necklaces. The charms include the house's signature logo and padlock, an airplane studded with diamonds, and a pink Papillon handbag in 18-karat gold and rose quartz. This last charm retails for $2,890.

Related Superstitions: Amber, Chai, Hamsa, Jade, Ladybug, Nazar Boncugu

11. 📷   CHINESE ASTROLOGY

General
Description:

In Chinese culture, a twelve-year cycle used to determine personality tendencies and compatibility factors for people born under each year's sign, akin to the Western Zodiac. Each year is assigned a sign that corresponds to a particular animal.

Origins:

The precise origins of the Chinese astrological system are unknown, although there are many folktales and legends to explain them. Astrology expert Neil Somerville recounts one myth in which the Buddha invited all the animals in his kingdom to celebrate the New Year. However, only twelve animals came to the Buddha's palace. Buddha then decided to name a year after each of the twelve animals and declared that people born in each of those years would inherit the qualities of that particular animal. The years run in cycles according to the order in which the animals arrived: rat, ox, tiger, rabbit, dragon, snake, horse, goat, monkey, rooster, dog, and pig.

Variations:

Those who are especially serious about their horoscopes divide history not into mere twelve-year cycles, but into sixty-year cycles. According to the longer cycle, each of the five sets of twelve years is further identified by one of the five elements—earth, fire, metal, water, and wood. Earth signs are disciplined, planned, grounded, and logical. Fire signs are emo-

tional and dramatic, charismatic leaders. Metal signs
are strong, stern, successful, and self-sufficient. Water
signs are subtle, go-with-the-flow types that may be
easygoing to the point of passivity. Wood signs have
solid foundations, are faithful friends, and tend to
experience personal growth and expansion, much as
trees develop rings over time.

In Practice: To determine your Chinese astrological sign, look up
your birthdate in one of the online databases or a
book on the topic. Because China follows a lunar calendar, the Chinese New Year falls on a day different
from that of the Gregorian calendar (used in the
West); therefore it is especially important for people
born in January and February to double check their
birthdates. Once you have determined your sign (and
your element, if you want the most complete information about your future), consult an expert. He or
she will provide you with a reading of your personality traits, the best times for you to make important
decisions, the signs with which you are compatible,
and advice on virtually any topic you feel will help
guide your decision making and destiny. Below is a
brief overview of the major characteristics of each sign.

• A **rat** is a perfectionist, a charmer who is generally
thrifty (but generous with family members), ambitious, and successful. The rat is a social butterfly but
ultimately family oriented.

- An **ox** is quiet, patient, and easy-going but has a tendency to be short tempered and stubborn. This person tends to be dedicated and hard working, often known to stay in one job for many years; not adventurous and prefers to stay close to home.

- A **tiger** is sensitive, deep, and graced with a courageous soul. However, this person can be notably indecisive and exhibits trouble with authority, tending to enter into conflicts somewhat easily.

- A **rabbit** boasts good financial skills, talent, and ambition. Rabbits make for good gamblers, but their generally conservative nature often prevents them from taking chances.

- A **dragon** is energetic and excitable, outgoing and eccentric, but also stubborn. Although they may have something of a hard shell, inside dragons are softies. Perhaps that is because they can rest easily at night, knowing they are born under a lucky sign.

- A **snake** is wise, quiet, and calm but can be vain and selfish; snakes tend to have particularly passionate inner lives. They are organized and responsible, particularly in financial matters, but they should never gamble, for they are notoriously poor at games of chance.

- A **horse** is a popular, happy person who does well in groups but can sometimes be too chatty and/or impatient. Generally elegant and eloquent, the horse excels in public speaking.

- A **goat** (sometimes called a ram) is shy and tends to be religious. Goats excel in the arts and can easily support themselves with their considerable talents. As with many artists, goats are laid-back and prefer an open schedule to a rigid routine.

- A **monkey** is an inventive, unique, ambitious character who may be something of a genius. Successful in most fields, monkeys prefer instant gratification and may at times lose out on long-term opportunities as a result. They are strong willed but able to relax before the onset of anger and real conflict.

- A **rooster** is achievement oriented. Roosters tend to be loners, exhibiting wild swings in both mood and fortune; as such they can be difficult partners and friends. Roosters are, however, well read and intelligent, well spoken, and talented in the art of debate.

- A **dog**, like their animal counterpart, is loyal, friendly, and honest and makes a naturally good leader. However, they are quick to find fault with others and can be stubborn about letting go of their ideas.

- A **pig** is loyal and friendly, like the dog, but is better at working with others and resolving problems. Pigs are also known to shy away from conflict and fighting.

Cultural Context:
The Chinese New Year is a major celebration not only in China but anywhere Chinese people live. Traditionally, the celebrations last two weeks, culminating in the famous Lantern Festival on the fifteenth of the month. On that day, elaborate lanterns illuminate the streets under a full moon. They provide dramatic lighting for the dragon dance, in which an enormous dragon, made of paper, silk, and other materials, is paraded through the streets. Red clothing and decorations are traditional for Chinese New Year celebrations since red is the color of fire, which drives away bad luck. Fireworks—in a range of fiery hues—are set off for the same reason.

Related Superstitions:
Astrological Horoscope

12.   **COMING AND GOING**

General Description:
The act of exiting a building via the same door through which you entered. This superstitious practice is thought to ensure that you will return in good health to that same structure.

Origins: 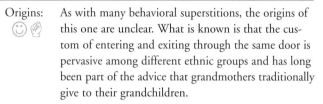 As with many behavioral superstitions, the origins of this one are unclear. What is known is that the custom of entering and exiting through the same door is pervasive among different ethnic groups and has long been part of the advice that grandmothers traditionally give to their grandchildren.

Variations: Other superstitions regarding comings and goings include painting a door red for the Chinese New Year (for good luck) or blue at any time (to ward off the evil eye); affixing a mezuzah to a doorframe and kissing it when entering and leaving a house or room (to ensure God's protection); opening the doors and windows of a house at the stroke of midnight on New Year's Eve to let the old year out and the new one in; opening the front door when a baby is being born; and hanging a lucky horseshoe over a doorway.

In Practice: When visiting friends and family, you must leave through the same door you entered to avoid bad luck. For example, if you attend a barbecue at a friend's house and enter through the front door but spend most of the afternoon in the backyard, at the end of the get-together you must reenter the house to exit through the front door. Simply circling outside from the backyard to the front of the house would not bode well for your friendship since doing so might indicate that you'll never return to the house.

| Cultural Context: | According to feng shui, the Chinese philosophy of organizing space to balance the energy of the persons living within it, one should use only one door for all comings and goings. Multiple entry and exit points will cause friction between the home's occupants and can lead to irreversible family problems. Furthermore, the front door should open only inward so that energy flows into the home. The back door should be used only to take out trash or enter the garden. Lastly, the front door should always be larger than the back door, and ideally the two doors should not be in sight of each other. |
| Related Superstitions: | Blue, Feng Shui, Horseshoe, Mezuzah |

13. 📷   **COW**

| General Description: ☺ | *A type of hoofed animal that is a member of the family Bovidae.* The cow is sacred in India, where it is a protected animal. Wooden and metal carvings of cows, often decorated with colorful wreaths of flowers and gold jewelry, are popular ornaments for Indian homes, to which they bring good luck. |
| Origins: ॐ | In the Hindu religion, Lord Krishna is said to have been incarnated as a cattle herder more than five thousand years ago. Krishna is known for having lifted a mountain to protect his cows. From these legends, |

Hindus determined that cows should be treated with the utmost reverence. In a largely vegetarian culture, this reverence makes sense. Cows are seen as motherly figures because they produce milk (not only a mainstay of the vegetarian diet but also used for ritual purposes in religious ceremonies), help till the soil, and provide essential fertilizers through their waste products.

In Practice: Because cows are free to roam as they please in India, they often survive thanks to the kindness of humans. It is considered lucky to feed a cow bread or fruit in the morning, but it is unlucky—in fact, it is illegal in much of the country—to harm or kill a cow. Thousands of illegal slaughterhouses exist, however, and some Indians are fighting the age-old religious and social taboos. Today, beef dishes appear increasingly on menus in many traditional Indian restaurants.

Cultural   Perhaps you have seen images of recumbent cows
Context: napping in the middle of busy New Delhi roads, as cars carefully circumnavigate the creatures so as not to disturb them. Indeed, there was once an Indian law stating that if one had to choose between hitting a cow and a human, it was preferable to hit the person. Today the presence of cows on major roadways in India is a cumbersome urban problem. As a first step in addressing the country's pressing issue of bovine population control, India now employs cow

catchers, contemporary "cowboys" specially trained to gently lure the animals off the streets and into vehicles that transport them to *gaushalas*, special cow reserves outside city limits. In these shelters, the cows are fed and cared for, milked, and given medical treatment.

Related Superstitions: Elephant

14. **CROSS**

General Description: *A replica of the wooden cross on which Jesus Christ was crucified, it is the primary symbol of Christianity.* It is a prominent feature in churches, homes, offices, and myriad other structures, both religious and secular. The cross consists of two planks—one vertical and one horizontal—placed at right angles to each other. The horizontal piece is typically shorter and located slightly above the center of the vertical piece (see icon, above left), although many variations exist. The crucifix includes a corpus, or replica of the body of Christ. Both are symbols of spirituality and protection.

Origins: The word *crucifix* is derived from the Latin *cruci fixus*, meaning "fastened to a cross." The form of a cross, however, existed long before the advent of Christianity or the death of Jesus Christ. Crosses have been found in ancient Egyptian hieroglyphs, where they appear most often as a T shape with a loop on the top, known as an "ansate" or "ankh" cross. This hieroglyph represented life and was alternately interpreted as a depiction of the joining of male and female genitalia and as a sandal thong with a loop around the ankle (the Egyptian words for *sandal* and *life* are similar). In addition, Stone Age sculptures in the shape of a cross have been discovered that date from 2000 BCE. In ancient Greece, the "tau" cross (shaped like the Greek letter T) was common. The cross was first used as a symbol of Christianity only in the time of Constantine I (ca. 280–337), the first Christian Roman emperor.

Variations: The hooked cross known as a swastika, also called a gamma, is today most closely associated with German Nazism in the West. Yet in fact, this equilateral cross has a long history as a good-luck symbol in the East and dates back to ancient Indian cultures. It is sacred in Hindu and Buddhist religions and can be found in Greek history as well. Pre-Nazi Europe interpreted the swastika as four intertwined Ls, representing luck, light, life, and love, and the symbol was often included in cards and gifts.

In Practice: A cross is used in Christian ceremonies, particularly those of the Catholic Church, to herald the Mass and remind worshippers of the sacrifice made by Jesus:

that of dying on the cross to save humanity from original sin. Many Christians decorate their homes with crucifixes, often hanging them above beds for protection and to facilitate religious education. The cross is thought to have the power to heal and ward off evil spirits.

Beyond the physical cross, Christians also make the sign of the cross during religious ceremonies as well as in moments of trial, prayer, and thanksgiving. In this ceremonial gesture, one holds together the right thumb, forefinger, and middle finger and then makes a cross by touching the forehead, then the heart, then each shoulder (the order of the shoulders differs in the Eastern and Western Churches). For some, it is common to kiss one's fingers at the completion of the motion, just as one might kiss a physical cross affixed to a rosary or other decorative prayer item. Crossing yourself is considered to be an effective means of blessing yourself or making sure that your prayers will be heard.

Cultural Context:

Those who believe in vampires also believe that a crucifix can be used to stave off these blood-sucking undead creatures. A cross alone will not do, however: To combat the vampire's evil forces, you must hold up a crucifix, complete with a replica of the body of Christ, and have complete faith in its healing and protective powers.

Related Superstitions:

Fingers Crossed, Garlic, Rosary

DESTINY

Other Name:	Fate.
General Description:	*The path predetermined for a person by a higher power, meaning that the person has no control over this path.* Destiny also presumes that the very concept of random luck doesn't exist because everything is preordained.
Origins:	Religions and traditions worldwide have long debated whether the universe is ruled by destiny or free will. Most human beings arrive at the conclusion that what they experience in life is a combination of both. Luck is, in essence, that very amalgamation. When we "get lucky," it is because we have done the right thing in the right place and made the right choice at the right time. At no time is everything in our lives under our complete control.
In Practice:	Soldiers talk about bullets with their names on them. Positive and negative events are seen as "meant to be" or as part of a "larger picture." Perhaps the most popular expression of destiny is the word *bashert*, a Yiddish term used in almost every imaginable context. Bashert is most often invoked when referring to love relationships. A Jewish tradition says that even before we are born, God determines who we are meant to marry by calling out that person's name just before we

exit the womb. The "near misses" of our love lives, our ex-lovers and ex-spouses, are said to be the souls who tried to compete with God at that very moment, calling out their names along with the name of the actual bashert. This belief is meant to explain why we sometimes feel drawn to more than one person or experience more than one meaningful love relationship. Human intellect cannot always distinguish between the echo, heard long ago, of other names and the voice of God announcing our one true love.

Cultural Context:
The catchphrase "manifest destiny" became popular in the United States during the mid-nineteenth century. This notion held that American expansion and development from the East Coast to the West Coast not only should happen, but certainly would happen. Proponents of manifest destiny expanded the idea to include American colonization of countries outside the United States, where they met with significant opposition.

Related Superstitions:
Destiny Number, Fates

DESTINY NUMBER

Other Name:
Soul number.

General
Description:

A numeral derived using the occult science of numerology by reducing the letters in an original birth name to a single digit that represents a person's ultimate tasks and cosmic destiny. Unlike a birth number, which describes a person's basic character traits and tendencies, the destiny number lays out a person's potential in life, considering the opportunities presented at birth. A destiny number signifies what you can achieve in this lifetime.

Origins:

Numerology is an occult science thought to date back to the ancient Greek mathematician Pythagoras (569–470 BCE). Other roots include the ancient Jewish mystic tradition called Kabbalah. Numerologists seek to find correlations between a person's significant numbers and the planets to which those numbers correspond. It is unknown who originally developed the concept of using the letters of a birth name to form the destiny number.

Variations:

Other numbers can be computed using the same numerical values. The soul urge number—the sum of the values of the vowels in your birth name—indicates your heart's desire, that is, the things that would make your life feel complete. The inner dream number—the sum of your name's consonant values—indicates your secret desires and fantasies (those you don't really need to live out but that signify key aspects of your psyche). Readings can also be made based on the day of the month on which you were born. Qualified numerologists will chart a full report based on any combination of these numbers.

In Practice: Different sources assign slightly different numerical values for the letters. The most common chart, known as the Pythagorean System of Numerology, calculates the following values:

Number	Corresponding Letters
1	A, J, S
2	B, K, T
3	C, L, U
4	D, M, V
5	E, N, W
6	F, O, X
7	G, P, Y
8	H, Q, Z
9	I, R

Add the numerical value of each letter in your first name and then reduce that sum to a single digit by adding the original digits. Repeat with middle names and family names. Then add the single-digit result of each name, reduce again, and the result will be another single digit that is your destiny number. For example, my name at birth was Alys Rho Yablon. When I add the value of the three names (3 + 5 + 6), the result is 14, which produces a destiny number of 5 (1 + 4 = 5). The number 5 signifies that my destiny has much to do with bringing about change and fighting for greater freedom, both on a personal and global level. Consult one of the many numerology books or Web sites to determine the significance of your own destiny number.

Be sure to take the original full given name, as written on your birth certificate. Married names or other legal name changes imposed after birth do not count, nor do nicknames, even if that is the name you are most commonly called.

Many parents who believe strongly in numerology will often consult experts before naming their children. They look for a number that represents worthwhile goals and is compatible with destiny numbers for the child's parents and other family members. Spellings of names should be scrutinized for optimal destiny number.

Cultural Context:

Numerology is popular in many cultures, especially contemporary Indian society. Abhishek Bachnan and Aishwarya Rai, the Bollywood couple who became engaged in 2007, made international headlines when they took extraordinary measures to align their astrological destinies. (Rai symbolically married a banana tree to transfer a curse inherent on her future spouse, as stated in her Vedic horoscope; see page 210.) The couple was advised about their destiny numbers as well. Although Western numerologists prefer the original birth name when calculating destiny numbers, the Indian handwriting and numerology expert Niraj Mancchanda predicted that Rai should assume her husband's surname after their marriage to ensure a better destiny number and, hence, a better marriage.

Related Superstitions:

Astrological Horoscope, Birth Number, Destiny, Master Numbers, Vedic Astrology

15. **DREAMCATCHER**

General Description:

A traditional Native American craftwork believed to filter dreams, allowing a person to benefit from good ones while protecting them from bad ones. The device consists of a circular hoop with a loose net or web woven inside. It is usually decorated with beads, feathers, and other ornaments.

Origins:

The dreamcatcher originated with the Ojibwe or Chippewa tribe of Native Americans. The Chippewa believe that spiders are associated with dreaming, and so they weave a dream-catcher net much as a spider weaves a web. The exact creation date of the first dreamcatcher is unknown; however, in the early twentieth century, the Chippewa began producing them in greater numbers, and other tribes soon followed. The dreamcatcher became a symbol of unity among various tribes and has become one of the more popular items sold in gift shops on American Indian reservations.

Variations: In Native American culture, feathers symbolize air and breath. Dreamcatchers are most often hung over Native American cradle boards, and the dangling feathers serve to entertain and stimulate the babies, who love watching the lightweight plumes dance in the wind. The feathers also provide a means of learning about air and wind, two of the major elements of life. Dreamcatchers for babies and children are made of willow and sinew; since both these materials disintegrate, they represent the fleeting nature of childhood, a temporary stage through which one passes on the way to adulthood. Dreamcatchers for adults are generally fashioned out of more weathered materials, such as aged fiber.

In Practice: This ornamental talisman is traditionally hung over beds to protect people from the evil forces of bad dreams, but it can also appear dangling from rearview mirrors, trees, and window frames. Hanging a dreamcatcher over a baby's cradle or young child's bed offers protection from the negative forces of bad dreams. It is believed that bad dreams will become caught in the netting and disappear when the sun rises while good dreams and positive thoughts will be filtered through the hole in the center of the web.

Cultural
Context:

Dreamcatcher meditation is a therapy designed for American Indian adolescents that aims to use the process of building a dreamcatcher as a means of exploring key psychological issues. The teens are given a kit consisting of a willow ring, a shuttle of string, feathers, and semiprecious stones. They are then led through the process of constructing their own dream-catcher as a supervisor conducts a meditation on Mother Earth. The participants are taught to meditate on the trees via the willow ring, on the air and water via the stones, on animal life via the feathers, and on the connectedness of all things and their part in the world via the string that forms the web.

16.

EGG

General
Description:

A female reproductive body; also, an embryo surrounded by nutritive matter and a hard, protective shell or outer covering. Since human beings (and birds, fish, insects, and so on) are born from eggs, these life-giving objects have come to represent health and creativity as well as the cycle of life.

Origins:

Which came first, the chicken or the egg? A timeless question, the origin of the egg remains a mystery. Its ovoid form is a ubiquitous symbol of life and fertility that has come to be associated with good luck in many diverse cultures.

In Practice:

† ✡ ♡

The painting of eggs for Easter celebrations is perhaps the best-known egg-based tradition in the West. The egg represents the rebirth of Jesus Christ, for even though a dormant egg may appear to be sleeping, within its shell new life waits to burst forth. The tradition stems from the legend of Mary Magdalene bringing a basket of eggs to the soldiers guarding the cross on which Christ was crucified. Mary cried in her attempts to lessen the soldier's cruelty, and her tears falling onto the eggs miraculously turned the shells different colors. In many countries, eggs were originally painted red on Easter to symbolize the blood of Christ. When making and hunting for Easter eggs became a more mainstream children's pastime, pastel colors and patterns gained popularity.

In Judaism, the egg has many purposes. On Passover, a hard-boiled egg is dipped in salt water as part of the Seder ritual, symbolizing new life born despite the tears shed by Hebrew slaves in Egypt. An egg is also eaten on the eves of Yom Kippur and Tisha B'Av, the two most solemn fast days of the Jewish calendar; they are sometimes sprinkled with ashes to remind people of the fragility of life. Finally, eggs are traditionally served in Jewish houses of mourning, representing the inevitable cycle of life from birth to death.

In China, new parents announce a baby's birth by hosting a "red egg and ginger" party, serving eggs dyed red in celebration of the new life. By contrast, a Japanese superstition holds that if a woman steps over an eggshell, she will go mad.

Do you want to find out who your one true love will be? According to folklore, if you boil an egg, remove and discard the yolk, fill the hollowed middle with salt, and eat it alone for dinner, that night you will dream of your future lover.

Cultural
Context:

Fabergé eggs—jeweled and enameled egg-shaped art-works first made by Russian artist Peter Carl Fabergé (1846–1920) for European royalty and private collectors—were originally intended as Easter eggs. The first Fabergé egg was designed in 1885 for the wife of Czar Alexander III, who was enthralled with the surprise held within (a golden "yolk"). For the next eleven years, a different egg was crafted especially for her on Easter. Each egg illustrated themes from Russian art throughout history and contained a delightful surprise. When Alexander died, his son Nicolas II continued the tradition, commissioning eggs to commemorate Russian landmarks (for example, the Trans-Siberian Railway) as well as famous figures and events. One of the most expensive is the Winter egg, designed in 1913. The jeweled masterpiece is made of two blocks of rock crystal and platinum and is studded with approximately three thousand rose-cut diamonds. The royal family paid 25,000 rubles for the egg in 1913 (roughly $12,500). In 1994 it was bought by an anonymous American businessman at a public auction for a record $5.5 million.

17.   **EIGHT AUSPICIOUS ARTICLES**

Other Name: *Ashtamangala.*

General
Description: *Eight symbols of good luck traditionally used in Buddhist
art.* They are a parasol, golden fish, right-spiraling
conch shell, victory banner, dharma wheel, endless
knot, lotus flower, and vase of treasure. The term *ashtamangala* comes from the Sanskrit *ashta* ("eight") and
mangala ("auspicious"). Along with the Buddhist religion, these symbols spread to the art of other Eastern
cultures, including China, India, Nepal, and Tibet.
The symbols represent progress along a person's spiritual path.

Origins: The symbols or articles developed along with the
Buddhist religions and correspond to key elements of
the Buddha's philosophy: divine protection, harmony,
inner wisdom, triumph over negativity, transformation, reconciliation of opposites, and enlightenment.

Variations: Buddhists further believe in eight auspicious sub-
stances that were presented as symbolic offerings to
the Buddha. These eight items correspond to the
eight-fold path of Buddhism: understanding (mirror),
thought (medicine), speech (curd), action (durva
grass), livelihood (bilva fruit), effort (right-spiraling
conch shell), mindfulness (vermillion powder), and
concentration (mustard seed).

In Practice: In addition to appearing frequently in Buddhist art, the eight auspicious articles are often worn as charms. Should you gather these symbols on a chain such as a bracelet, it is important to consider the meaning of each of the following:

• The **parasol** stands for protection from illness and hardship. Long recognized as a symbol of power and wealth, the parasol protects its owner from harsh sunlight and inclement weather. It also represents the protective powers of the Buddha, who shelters and safeguards the faithful.

• A pair of fish whose heads meet, the **golden fish** represent peace and harmony. In the Buddhist tradition, the sea is a symbol of fear and suffering. Because fish swim without worry of drowning or being carried away by currents, they are seen as particularly brave and carefree, and their freedom should be emulated.

• The **right-spiraling conch shell** represents the deep, echoing sounds of the Buddha's teachings and inner wisdom. Right-leaning movement is especially auspicious because the Buddha's hairs are depicted in a spiral that curves to the right, and the sun, moon, planets, and stars appear to move to the right around the earth.

• The **victory banner** is symbolic of the triumph of mind and body over negativity as well as the victory of Buddhist thought. It is considered a major accomplishment to triumph over the four major hurdles in life: emotional confusion, passion, fear of death, and pride and lust. When we move past these obstacles, we are victorious indeed.

- The **dharma wheel**, or *dharmachakra*, is a central symbol of Buddhism. Composed of a circular rim (symbolizing limitation), eight spokes (corresponding to the eight-fold path), and a central axis that reminds us of the physical realm in which we are grounded, the dharma wheel illustrates the process of transformation and learning.

- The **endless knot** is a series of intertwined lines joined at right angles to form a closed pattern. This image symbolizes the opposition of forces in life (secular and religious, wisdom and compassion, and so on) and the need to reconcile them to achieve inner balance.

- The ultimate sign of enlightenment, the **lotus flower** is a ubiquitous Buddhist symbol representing purification and the blossoming of awareness. The plant takes root in the mud, stretches through the water, and eventually emerges and blooms above the water's surface—thus undergoing every stage of personal development and, literally, achieving light.

- The **vase of treasure** is not just a symbol of monetary wealth but of long life, health, and the intangible riches of knowledge and satisfaction that come with the study of the Buddha's wisdom.

Cultural Context:

The lotus flower also figures as an important symbol in Egyptian mythology. Ancient Egyptians believed that the sun god emerged from the lotus flower of the primordial waters. Therefore they considered the lotus to be a symbol of the sun and of rebirth since the flower closes and sinks below the water's surface at night and reemerges and blossoms again in the morning. Egyptian funerary texts known as *The Book of the Dead* even include a spell one can use to turn oneself into a lotus to achieve resurrection.

Related Superstitions:

Charm Bracelet, Goddess Lakshmi, Laughing Buddha

18. **ELEPHANT**

General Description:

☺

A large, herbivorous mammal of the family Elephantidae native to tropical Africa and southeast Asia. This elegant, intelligent animal is famous for its elongated, muscular trunk; ivory tusks; and large, flapping ears (Asian elephants have smaller ears). Now protected animals, only three major species of elephants survive; many became extinct, largely because of the ivory

trade. Elephants have the longest gestation of any animal—twenty-two months—and at birth a calf can
weigh up to 250 pounds (113 kg). A common source
of entertainment in historical and contemporary circuses, the elephant is considered a lucky animal.

Origins: Ganesha, the Hindu god of luck, has the head of an
ॐ   elephant atop a human body. The notion of the lucky
            elephant gained popularity in the United States and
            Europe during the British colonization of the Indian
            subcontinent in the 1700s. In the 1930s, the lucky
            elephant reached its zenith. Americans determined
            that only "trunk-up" figurines were definitively lucky.
            The legendary white elephant of Thailand also
            informed the American fascination with elephants.

Variations: The white elephant is one of the Buddha's many
☸   incarnations, and its image is used in Buddhist art to
               denote royalty and divinity. The rarity of the white
               elephant gives it a special aura, and the animals are
               especially revered in Thailand.

In Practice: To bring good luck and protection to a household,
🤚   place near the doorframe of the front door small statues
                or sculpted figurines of elephants holding their trunks
                high in the air. The elephant symbolizes strength, wis-
                dom, loyalty, and intelligence—all qualities one desires
                in a family.

                Ironically, many "lucky elephants" are carved from

ivory, the very material that is responsible for the untimely and cruel death of the animal. If you want to celebrate the auspicious nature of the elephant, do not support the ivory trade. Instead, find an elephant carved from stone, jade, or a synthetic material.

Cultural
Context:

Elephant rides are popular attractions at circuses and fairs. In addition, elephants are used as ceremonial mounts for religious rituals, and they serve as the primary means of transportation for adventurous safari-goers. Throughout Asia and Africa, brides and grooms are sometimes announced on the back of a decorated elephant. In Thailand, elephants are the ultimate symbol of the land. They help transport heavy logs and timber and are sturdy mounts for people trekking through treacherous trail areas. Once featured on the Thai national flag, the animals are often decorated and paraded through the streets for special occasions.

Related
Superstitions:

Goddess Lakshmi

19.   **EVIL EYE**

General
Description:

The intentional or unintentional gaze of a person who is jealous of what another has gained. When good things happen to you, beware: You may be in danger of a nefarious force manifested in this gaze, which is feared throughout the world. It is believed there are three types of evil eyes: unconscious, deliberate, and invisible. An evil eye may be cast upon you by someone who is particularly envious of your possessions or relationships; who wishes ill will upon you; or whose praise may ultimately be construed in a negative or potentially harmful way, as in a backhanded compliment. Whether or not the evil eye was cast upon you deliberately or unconsciously, its effects can be disastrous, even deadly. To repel the eye or repair damages already done, many cultures invoke varied spells, talismans, and physical responses (see "In Practice").

Origins: References to the evil eye can be found in the Old and New Testaments (some say that the tenth commandment, "Thou shalt not covet," refers to the evil eye) as well as in Sumerian, Babylonian, and Assyrian texts dating to approximately 3000 BCE.

Variations: In Semitic countries throughout the Middle East and Mediterranean, people with fair skin and blue eyes are considered to be especially dangerous. The unusual eye color frightens some superstitious people, and the result is that blue-eyed persons are treated with particular distrust. In India, women began to wear dark kohl around their eyes and apply red lipstick not only to deflect the evil eye but also to help themselves lest they be inclined to inflict the maleficent gaze either verbally or visually.

In Practice: There are many ways to ward off the evil eye. These include spitting, knocking on wood, uttering specific phrases in various languages, holding onto your favorite talisman, or wearing charms. You can almost always find a way to avert the negative power of jealous attentions (see "Cultural Context," below). In India, red chilies and camphor are burned to divert the evil eye.

Cultural Context: Grandmothers are perhaps the most inclined to be concerned about the evil eye, especially when their grandchildren are concerned. A Jewish grandmother might say, "My son the doctor has three beautiful girls, each one more gorgeous than the next—*keyn aynohorah* [Yiddish for 'there should be no evil eye']." A Christian grandmother might be prone to knocking on the nearest hard surface when mentioning her grandson, who happens to be a genius. A Greek grandmother may spit three times upon learning that her granddaughter was accepted at Harvard Law School, and a Muslim grandmother might say, "Mash'Allah," Arabic for "God has willed it." A Moroccan grandmother might not say (or spit) anything at all, preferring to finger the hamsa charm on her necklace and whisper, "Hamsa, hamsa, hamsa!"

Related Superstitions: Blue, Garlic, Hamsa, Henna, Knocking on Wood, Nazar Boncugu, Red String, Spitting, Voodoo Dolls

20. ⊙   **FATES**

General
Description: *Three Greek goddesses who control the destinies of all beings, both mortal and immortal.* In Greek mythology, the Fates were known as the *Moirae*, or "apportioners." They were sisters, and each had a different role. Clotho, the spinner, was present at a person's birth and spun the thread of life. Lachesis, the allotter, determined the length of that thread, measuring it according to her prophecy. Atropos, the inevitable, cut the thread at the end of a person's life, thus determining the moment of death.

Origins: Also known as the Moirae, the Fates are major figures in Greek mythology. There are various theories to explain their parentage. One popularly held belief is that they are the offspring of Zeus and Themis, the goddess of necessity.

Variations: The Romans called the Fates the Parcae, and the three sisters were known as Nona, Decuma, and Morta. Moira, a popular Gaelic name, is derived from *Moirae* and translates as "bitter." The Hebrew name Miriam means "bitter sea."

In Practice: Women in labor may call out to the goddess Clotho in the hope that their babies will soon be delivered. Clotho answers, spinning her thread, and the infant enters the world. Lachesis then takes over, deciding the length of that particular being's existence, his or her experiences, and life events. She measures out the string and follows it to its inevitable end. Lachesis then holds the thread for Atropos, who cuts it, symbolizing the end of the life begun with Clotho's intervention.

Cultural Context:

The Fates are featured in Homer's *Odyssey*. Depicted as three old, ugly hags (sometimes with beards), they were as powerful as they were unattractive—and widely feared. The modern word *spinster* is derived from the concept of these three single women with no clear familial links who spun out, and then cut, the thread of life.

The Fates have appeared in countless works of art and literature throughout the ages. Yet perhaps the most famous allusion is in Shakespeare's masterpiece *Macbeth*. In the play, three "weird sisters" prophesy in their peculiar rhyme, foretelling the fate of Macbeth that leads to his insanity. The witchlike sisters act as the main characters of several scenes, setting the play's eerie tone: "Fair is foul and foul is fair. / Hover through the fog and filthy air." The modern word *weird* is derived from the Old English *wyrd*, meaning "fate." It is therefore assumed that the three weird sisters are allusions to the Moirae of Greek mythology.

Related Superstitions:

Destiny, Karma

FENG SHUI

General Description:
☺♡

An ancient Chinese philosophy that promotes the organization of living space or workspace as a means of channeling a person's life energy. Made up of complex rules regarding the arrangement and placement of furniture and objects in every room of a home or office, feng shui attempts to balance the forces of yin and yang, thus resulting in a greater sense of inner peace and fulfillment. It consists of an intricate system of patterns for everything from furniture and plants to doors, windows, crystals, and paint color. Adherents of feng shui believe that by avoiding certain objects and incorporating others into a decor, you can change the energy of the physical environment and improve the inhabitant's luck in life, love, and business.

Origins:

Literally translated from the Chinese for "wind" and "water," feng shui is a concept inherent in Taoism, a religious tradition that dates to prehistoric China. It embodies the idea that all energy (*chi*) is carried by the wind and contained within water. Because everything is considered to be a manifestation of chi, it is crucial that chi be allowed to flow properly. Energy that flows incorrectly or is blocked will impede the balance of any person living within that space. Today the philosophy extends to architectural design, landscape art, and psychology.

In Practice: The fundamental principle of feng shui is to balance your personal energy by properly balancing objects surrounding you. Clutter is the ultimate energy blocker, and it hinders one's success in all aspects of daily life. For example, by cleaning your desk, you will clear your head, making room for success at work. Everything must occupy its proper space. Find that space and you'll find the energy that's lost in the mess.

If you have an office, never sit with your back to the door; in doing so, you turn your back on opportunity. Mirrors make helpful additions because they attract money, as do bright colors painted on walls and wind chimes hung from the ceiling.

Unlike office chairs, beds should never be arranged so that your feet directly face the door. Sleeping in such a position will pull the energy you gained in sleep away from you and out of the room. Mirrors in a bedroom are also said to drain your energies, and dark colors are not recommended. The bed's headboard should always be set firmly against a wall to ground you and provide a sense of security. Pink and red tones are beneficial for romance, silver and gold for general luck. For couples, matching sets of lamps or bedside tables are good omens of harmony and equality, as are pictures taken at happy moments.

Feng shui can extend even to the bathroom. There, the toilet seat should be kept down and the sink drain covered with a plug when not in use. If left exposed, drains are thought to wash away money and good health.

The front door of a house should be clearly marked, without plants blocking the entryway and with a clean walkway leading to it. Wind chimes, natural sunlight, and open space in the foyer are the best arbiters of good luck for the house as a whole. Plants are good, in general, although bright overhead lights are bad. Exposed beams should be avoided everywhere in a house but especially in the bedroom, because they can divide the energy of the room and disrupt communication among the inhabitants.

Cultural Context:
Feng shui is more popular than ever, in the East and West alike. The current interest in New Age philosophies and techniques has seen the proliferation of feng shui schools and training courses throughout the world, and countless books have been published on the topic. Feng shui experts are hired for one-on-one consultations about all types of spaces, from private homes and work cubicles to corporate offices, commercial hotels, and resort complexes. Some consultants may focus on the popular, more superficial aspects of feng shui; others have trained seriously and study the intricacies of Chinese philosophy, numerology, architecture, design, and environmental and industrial psychology.

Related Superstitions:
Chinese Astrology, Coming and Going, Gourd, I Ching

21. FINGERS CROSSED

General
Description:

The gesture by which one's middle finger is crossed and hooked over the index finger (or vice versa) as a harbinger of good luck, a reversal of bad luck, and a repellant of evil spirits. It is also used as a means of waiting out uncertain times while wishing for the best possible outcome.

Origins:

Although "fingers crossed" generally symbolizes the desire for good luck, it is most commonly believed to be a physical emulation of the Christian cross.

In Practice:

The act of crossing fingers often has religious connotations, similar to making the sign of the cross (see page 59), by recalling the crucifix on which Christ died. People hope that the powers of Jesus Christ will protect them or grant wishes. Furthermore, crossing one's fingers takes less time and is less conspicuous than making the sign of the cross. It may be a preferable expression when time is of the essence; when discretion is necessary; or when faced with a traumatic encounter with evil.

Today much of our communication is remote, such as talking over the phone or sending e-mail or text messages. Therefore, many people replace the physical act of crossing fingers with saying or typing the phrase, as in, "I'm waiting to hear back about my application to Harvard. Fingers crossed!"

Cultural
Context:

Instead of using the "fingers crossed" gesture to attract good things, some people use it as a sneaky way to avoid something bad or to trick someone. Most common is crossing your fingers behind your back while telling a white lie. This act is believed to save the liar from spending an eternity in hell.

Related
Superstitions:

Cross, Evil Eye

22.   **FISH**

General
Description:

An aquatic vertebrate often covered in scales and equipped with gills that allow it to breathe underwater. Fish are a vital food source for people, animals, and other marine life. Perhaps because of this reason, they have also served as a popular subject in art and literature, appearing in varied works by cultures worldwide, from ancient Egyptian and Greek wall paintings to Micronesian textiles to the twentieth-century American novel *Jaws*.

Origins:
☺

Many cultures revere fish, though it is unclear when they first became linked with good luck. Fishlike beings appear in ancient Greek mythology in the form of Sirens. These half-woman half-fish creatures endowed with supernatural powers are the precursors of the more modern notion of the mermaid.

The fish also has a long history as a religious symbol, notably the appropriation of the ichthys (from the ancient Greek word for fish) by early Christians beginning in the first century CE and continuing today. Fish are mentioned several times in the gospels of the Christian Bible, making it a natural symbol for the early followers of Jesus to have adopted. The so-called Jesus fish consists of two intersecting arcs whose ends extend slightly to create a fishlike shape.

Over the centuries, the fish has also become associated with the Jewish holiday of Rosh Hashana (the Jewish New Year). In addition, Buddhism's Eight Auspicious Articles include an image of two fish facing each other. The science of astrology uses it as the symbol for Pisces. The Chinese word for fish, *yu*, rhymes with the Chinese word for luck, *fu*. Because of this coincidence, the Chinese consider fish to be a good luck symbol.

In Practice: The ichthys has seen renewed popularity, popping up on cars as bumper stickers and decals or hanging on walls in Christian homes and houses of worship. The image may feature a cross in the place of the fish's eye and contain the word "Jesus" within. Evolutionists have appropriated the image, adding feet to the fish and replacing Jesus' name with that of Darwin, a reference to Charles Darwin's theory of evolution.

A fish is also considered to be a harbinger of wisdom, so eating one is believed to impart knowledge to the consumer. In China, it is considered auspicious to be presented with (and eat) a whole fish at a dinner party or a New Year's celebration. The whole fish is generally presented at the end of the meal, symbolizing that endings are also beginnings of new stages of life, and it is served pointing toward the guest of honor. This custom may explain why so many Chinese restaurants incorporate fishponds into their decor. During the Jewish holiday of Rosh Hashana, only the head of a fish is presented to the head of the household, who makes a special blessing before eating part of it and sharing it with those in attendance: "May it be your [God's] will that we be like the head [the leader] and not like the tail [the follower]." Because fish cannot close their eyes, the fish head is a sign of awareness and knowledge, two traits one hopes to acquire during a new year. Another way to obtain the luck or wisdom this water-dwelling creature imparts is to wear a fish charm.

Cultural Context:

Omega-3 fatty acids, also known as polyunsaturated fatty acids, are one of the key nutrients found in fish. As numerous studies have shown, Americans tend to ingest far less of this nutrient than they should, mainly because they do not maintain diets high in fresh fish, fruits, and vegetables. Taking an omega-3 supplement (or simply eating more fish) has proved to be effective in reducing the inflammation that leads to cardiovascular disease. It has also been shown to help prevent such diseases as arthritis, stroke, diabetes, osteoporosis, depression, and certain cancers. Pregnant women take extra omega-3 vitamins to ensure the healthy development of the fetuses' brains.

Related
Superstitions: Astrological Horoscope, Charm Bracelet, Eight Auspicious Articles

23.   **FORTUNE COOKIE**

General
Description: *A thin, crisp sugar cookie shaped like a half moon, inside of which is a piece of paper containing a fortune, a list of lucky numbers, and sometimes a lesson in Chinese language (usually a word or phrase).* Accompanied by the bill at the end of a meal in Chinese restaurants, the fortune cookie is often served with orange slices and a pot of tea. It is a well-known treat worldwide but enjoys special popularity in America.

Origins: Contrary to popular belief, the fortune cookie did not originate in China. In fact, it was invented in the early twentieth century by a restaurateur in San Francisco, California, making it an entirely American enterprise. There is not even a Chinese word for this fortune-bearing treat.

In Practice: You've likely dined in a Chinese restaurant, enjoying the tasty egg rolls, chicken and snow peas, pork-fried rice, and Szechwan eggplant. Upon finishing your meal, your server arrives with a plate of fortune cookies and orange slices. You should close your eyes and choose a cookie at random, knowing that the right fortune will find you. Once you've selected, slowly break the cookie in half and reveal the small, white paper hidden inside. Placed between two smiley faces will be your fortune, along with a string of lucky numbers and a Chinese phrase and its translation.

Because fortune cookies are generally taken with a grain of salt (that is, they are not considered to be a particularly accurate prediction of one's future), much fun is had at their expense. The most popular game is to add the phrase "in bed" to the end of the fortune. For example, the rather tame and vague statement "Friendship is the key to happiness" becomes the much more suggestive "Friendship is the key to happiness in bed."

Another fun activity associated with fortune cookies involves making a marriage proposal. Some men have asked their girlfriends to marry them by having the server at the couple's favorite Chinese restaurant bring her a fortune cookie with the important question "Will you marry me?" hiding within its folds.

Cultural Context: ☺

In a landmark windfall of good luck, 110 people claimed second-prize-winning tickets (collection amounts ranging from $100,000 to $500,000) in the U.S. Powerball lottery drawing of March 30, 2005. All 110 winners had played the same numbers—22, 28, 32, 33, and 39—just missing the powerball number that would have made them grand-prize winners. Such a large number of winners with identical numbers was unprecedented in U.S. lottery history. An investigation revealed that the winners had in fact played numbers they had received in fortune cookies. Because those fortunes are mass-produced and distributed nationwide, hundreds of cookies with the same combination of numbers were floating around at just the right time. The cookies were traced to Wonton Food, Inc., a factory in Queens, New York.

Related
Superstitions: Fortune-Teller

24.   **FORTUNE-TELLER**

General
Description: *A person who consults with spirits, higher forces, crystal
                balls, and tarot cards; who reads palms; or who references
                the zodiac, runes, or other magical devices in an effort to
                prophesy the future of a client.* A fortune-teller inter-
                prets the life and spiritual energy of the client and tai-
                lors predictions to his or her specific questions. The
                fortune-teller may be imbued with a special talent
                known as ESP (extrasensory perception), which allows
                the clairvoyant to see more deeply into the nature of
                the universe and predict the future.

Origins: Fortune-telling has long been associated with so-called
                Gypsy cultures, although divination has been part of
                societies worldwide since ancient times. Some form of
                fortune-telling has likely always existed. It appears in
                nearly every known culture, from ancient Greek ora-
                cles, Chinese oracle bones, and Druid runes to dream
                interpretations in the Bible, I Ching, and Kabbalah.

Variations: You may prefer to serve as your own clairvoyant.
                Embark on becoming an expert in tarot cards, astrology,
                numerology, Ouija boards, or crystals. An even
                quicker, and less expensive, option is to purchase a
                Magic-8 Ball. Shaped like a billiard ball, this "div-
                ination" toy is equipped with a clear plastic window
                through which you see a white, plastic, twenty-sided
                die floating in blue liquid. Each side of the die is
                inscribed with an answer. To use, simply ask the ball
                an important question, shake it, and turn it so that
                the window faces you. The answer will magically rise
                to the surface. Be prepared for such revelatory and
                helpful responses as, "Try Again," "You bet!" "No
                Way!" and "Absolutely."

In Practice: Fortune-tellers come in all shapes and sizes and
                employ a number of different methods to predict the
                future. They are most commonly found in urban set-
                tings and are generally consulted for the purpose of
                amusement. However, some clairvoyants are sought
                after by those who are especially concerned about

determining the course of their future. Some people will go so far as to hire a personal psychic (or call one via a 900 phone number) to read into every life event and disclose its far-reaching significance.

A stereotypical image of a fortune-teller usually shows a middle-aged woman (or, less frequently, a wizardlike man). She has a dark complexion and long, red-painted nails, is cloaked in layered scarves and colorful, flowing skirts, and wears jingling bangles and dangling earrings. She usually sits in a mysterious, tentlike space, dimly illumined by candles and decorated with ominous pictures and colorful wall hangings. The client sits opposite the fortune-teller, often close to the ground, likely on pillows rather than on a chair. The fortune-teller may read the client's palms or consult tarot cards, or she may simply gaze into a crystal ball until falling into a trancelike state, from which she may conjure spirits of dead relatives or view similar supernatural specters.

If you consult a psychic via the Internet or telephone, be prepared for an overly general reading. It may sound something like the following: "I sense someone named John in your life" or "You may have a problematic relationship with someone" or "You are searching for something." Be warned: These generalities can cost you—sometimes as much as several dollars per minute. So talk fast!

Cultural
Context:

In the 1988 movie *Big*, Tom Hanks plays Josh Baskin, a preteen who is sick of being a kid. At a carnival, a sullen Josh inserts a quarter into a pinball-type machine in which resides the figure of a fortune-teller. The mechanical wizard raises his head, his eyes open and exude light, and a message lights up saying, "Zoltar Says: Make your wish." Josh complies, saying he wishes to be "big," a grown-up. The next morning, he wakes up in an adult body, albeit one that has retained the mind of a twelve-year-old boy. The story that follows is one of American cinema's classics: Josh becomes a successful executive at a toy company after his uncanny ability to know what kids want propels him to the top of the corporate ladder. Ultimately, the complexities of adult life overwhelm him, and Josh tracks down Zoltar to reverse his fortune and become a child again, thus proving the old adage: Be careful what you wish for.

According to New York State Penal Law 165.35, fortune-telling is a class B misdemeanor. The law reads: "A person is guilty of fortune telling when, for a fee or compensation which he directly or indirectly solicits or receives, he claims or pretends to tell fortunes, or holds himself out as being able, by claimed or pretended use of occult powers, to answer questions or give advice on personal matters or to exorcise, influence or affect evil spirits or curses; except that this section does not apply to a person who engages in the aforedescribed conduct as part of a show or exhibition solely for the purpose of entertainment or amusement." In 1999 this law gained significant press when the New York Police Department's Fraud Squad conducted a sting operation known as "Operation Crystal Ball." They arrested a Manhattan fortune-teller who billed a client for $50,000, claiming to be the only one capable of lifting a curse that had been placed on her.

Related
Superstitions:
Astrological Horoscope, Birth Number, Destiny Number, Fortune Cookie, I Ching, Ouija Board, Palm Reading, Runes, Tarot Cards

25.   **FOUR-LEAF CLOVER**

General
Description:
☺
A rare occurrence, the four-leaf clover is a genetic muta-
tion of the more common three-leaf white clover plant
(Trifolium repens). The three-leaf clover, also known as a shamrock, is the symbol of Ireland and all things Irish, so the four-leaf clover is similarly associated with that country and the "luck of the Irish." It is considered to be a universal symbol of good luck, and finding one in a field bodes well for its discoverer.

Origins:
It is unclear exactly when the four-leaf clover became associated with good luck, but it is first mentioned as early as the Middle Ages. In the seventeenth century, white clover was used as a good-luck charm among the Celtic people of Wales as well as the Druids.

Variations: According to Philippa Waring, author of the
               Dictionary of Omens and Superstitions, finding a four-
               leaf clover is a sign that you will meet your true love
               the same day. If you give the clover to someone else
               that day, your luck increases. She also notes that, in
               times of war, wearing a four-leaf clover in your lapel
               will prevent you from being drafted.

In Practice: One in ten thousand clovers has four leaves. If you
               are lucky enough to find one in a field, you are
               advised to guard and preserve it, for you may never
               find one again. If you are impatient and don't think
               you can spend endless days scouring meadows and
               counting leaves, you can still acquire the plant's luck.
               Charms, jewelry, keychains, and other replications of
               the clover are available worldwide. Some people
               believe that having one in your home or vehicle will
               help protect you and attract positive energy.

Cultural   In Catholic Ireland, the shamrock's standard three
Context: leaves represent the Holy Trinity—Father, Son, and
   †   Holy Ghost. A fourth leaf is especially auspicious
               because it symbolizes God's grace. This interpretation
               is connected to the symbol as it is used on St.
               Patrick's Day, the holiday celebrated on March 17.
               Because St. Patrick, Ireland's patron saint, is said to
               have brought Christianity to that country in the
               fourth century, thus helping reform the pagan Druids,
               he is associated with this fourth leaf and its deeper

religious symbolism. St. Patrick used the three-leaf shamrock to illustrate the concept of the Trinity to his students, so another tradition of St. Patrick's Day is to pray for the success of missionaries worldwide.

The four-leaf clover is also the symbol of the 4-H Club, an international youth leadership program whose name stands for "head, heart, hands, and health." It is also one of the more popular marshmallow shapes in Lucky Charms cereal from General Mills. (The other marshmallow shapes are hearts, moons, stars, horse-shoes, pots of gold, rainbows, and red balloons.)

Related Superstitions: Charm Bracelet, Heather, Luck of the Irish

FRIDAY THE THIRTEENTH

General Description: *When the thirteenth day of the month falls on a Friday, beware.* This day has "bad luck" written all over it. It is inauspicious to be born, get married, start a new job, or cut your fingernails on any Friday the thir-teenth. The fear of this day is so prominent that today there is an official name for the phobia: paraskevidekatria. Fear of the number thirteen alone is called triskaidekaphobia.

Origins: Both Friday as a day of the week and thirteen as a number are considered bad luck on their own. Only in the twentieth century did the notion of Friday the thirteenth come to have specifically negative associations. The most commonly believed origins for these beliefs are linked to Christianity: Jesus Christ was crucified on a Friday, and thirteen people (Jesus and his twelve apostles) attended the Last Supper.

Aside from the strong Christian associations, Fridays were also known in England and Rome as "Hangman's Day," since that was the weekday on which criminals were publicly hanged. According to Norse traditions, there are twelve demigods. Adding the evil spirit, Satan, brings that number to an inauspicious thirteen.

Other origins of the fear of this day and date relate to the Christian/pagan divide. Friday was known as the "witches' Sabbath," and witches were known to travel in covens of twelve. When joined by the devil to form a group of thirteen, they were believed to wreak havoc on the world.

Variations: In Greece and Spain, Tuesday the thirteenth is unlucky, not Friday. Many Greeks associate this weekday with an unfortunate event: It was on a Tuesday, in 1453, that the city of Constantinople fell to the Ottoman Empire. In Spanish culture, Tuesday is *Martes*, from the root *Mars*, the god of war. For these reasons, many in these cultures consider Tuesdays, when combined with the unlucky number 13, to be especially inauspicious.

In Practice:	Despite the separate histories of Friday and the number thirteen, this day of the month as a unit has become linked to "Murphy's Law," which states that "whatever can go wrong, will go wrong." The fear of this day is so pronounced that businesses project millions of dollars in lost revenue when the thirteenth day of a month falls on a Friday.

If you are truly afraid of Friday the thirteenth, avoid travel and any other activity that may be potentially dangerous and do not start anything significant that day. If you can, schedule a "personal day" and stay home from work. You will be better able to avoid exterior dangers, but you should take extra precautions as well. Draw the curtains and avoid cooking, lest you cut yourself with a knife, burn yourself on the stove, or experience a gas leak, an electrical short-circuit, or a run-in with the Devil himself.

Cultural Context:	Perhaps the most familiar cultural reference to this superstition is the series of horror movies that began with 1980's *Friday the 13th*. In these films, the ghost of Jason returns to Camp Crystal Lake (where he drowned as a child) to murder counselor after counselor in increasingly horrific ways. The murders usually occur on Friday the thirteenths. These landmark horror sequels have captivated scary-movie fans for more than two decades, contributing to the widespread fear of the horrible, bloody things that can happen on that fateful day.

26.   **FROG**

General
Description: *Amphibious creatures that live partly on land, partly in
☺ ✿   water.* In many cultures, these small green reptiles are
associated with good luck, fertility, and miraculous
transformation.

Origins: In Japan, frogs are symbols of safe returns for travelers
and also of financial returns. Because frogs tend to
croak the loudest before and during a rainstorm, the
Japanese consider them gods of rain and good harvest.
In America, frogs are associated with money because
of their green color. In other cultures, frogs are linked
to fertility not only because they lay a large number
of eggs (about 1,500 at a time) but also because of
their incredible independent growth, from tiny tad-
poles to fully formed frogs.

Variations: It is a common myth that frogs cause warts. But
another myth says that rubbing your skin with a frog
will cure warts. Scientifically, neither belief is true.
Warts are caused by the human papilloma virus
(HPV), which can be contracted only from other
humans. According to Dr. Robert Shmerling, however,
one frog-based medical superstition may be true. It

has long been said that frogs can cause mental illness. It turns out that frogs do produce certain chemical compounds that are toxic to the human nervous system. If ingested, this toxin can cause hallucinations.

In Practice: Replicas of frogs, from bejeweled charms to silly statues, are popular gifts worldwide. Place one in your wallet to remind the exiting banknotes to return as soon as possible, in your car to ensure a safe journey, or near your bed for increased fertility. Single women may also want to carry a frog at all times, but particularly on blind dates, as a reminder that eventually their prince will come (see "Cultural Context," below).

Cultural Context: The Brother's Grimm fairytale "The Frog Prince" is one of the most beloved and often-interpreted stories of all time. In the original tale, one day a spoiled princess is playing by a well, throwing her favorite toy, a gold ball, into the air and catching it. When the ball accidentally falls into the well, the princess is inconsolable. Wailing, she proclaims that she would give all her riches just to have her ball back, whereupon a frog answers her from inside the well. If she will promise to love him and live with him and be his companion, he will get the ball for her—she need not give him any riches. The princess, assuming that the frog will never make it beyond his little well, hastily agrees, and the frog indeed fishes the ball out of the well for her. Overjoyed, the princess grabs the ball and runs back to her castle, leaving the poor frog alone in his well.

Later than night, the frog makes his way to the castle and demands his due. He wants to eat off the golden plates of the princess and be taken to her room to sleep on her pillow. Although initially the princess refuses, her father, the king, insists that she keep her word. Begrudgingly, she does as she is told. That night, the frog demands to lie in bed with her, and in anger she throws him against the wall. In the morning, she awakens to find not the ugly frog but a handsome prince, who informs her that they are to be married.

This less-than-romantic tale has been softened over the years into the more popular story of a grateful princess who kisses the frog in thanks for his good deed, upon which he magically turns into a prince. The prince, who was cursed by an angry witch because of his hubris, has been waiting for his one true love, the beautiful princess, to restore him to his original form. That can happen only once the princess loves him for his good deeds (as a frog) rather than his good looks (as a prince). Everyone lives happily ever after and learns an invaluable lesson about inner beauty. It is this version of "The Frog Prince" that has made its way into children's stories today and forms the basis for the saying among single women that "you have to kiss a lot of frogs before you find your prince."

Related Superstitions: Making a Wish, Wishing Well

27. 📷 **FULL MOON**

General
Description:

The phase of the lunar cycle during which the moon is on the opposite side of the earth from the sun, such that it is in full view. When this view occurs, the moon is fully illuminated by the sun and appears as a large, glowing circle in the night sky. A full moon occurs roughly every 29 1/2 days.

Origins:
☹

Long associated with bad luck, insanity, insomnia, werewolves, and zombies, the evening of the full moon is also referred to as the "night of the living dead." The exact origins of its inauspicious connotations are difficult to determine. In superstitious times and places, the eerie half-light created by a full moon, compared to the relative darkness during other times in the lunar cycle, certainly contributed to apprehension and fear. In medieval times, parents were told to make sure their daughters did not walk near open windows with their hair down, since demons would be better able to see them in the moonlight and could enter their homes through the girls' hair.

In Practice:

Perhaps the most common manifestation of the danger inherent in the full moon is the appearance of the mythical werewolf. Half man, half wolf, a werewolf comes out only on the night of a full moon. Once cursed with the werewolf blood (after being scratched or bitten or through a biological tie), were-people will turn into werewolves under the light of the full moon—their hair grows longer, their eyes turn red or yellow, their teeth grow to massive canine proportions, and their nails become vicious claws. The only way to cure a werewolf is to shoot it with a silver bullet. If you do not have one on hand, be sure to stay indoors on the night of a full moon, especially if you live near the woods or think you hear the unmistakable sound of a wolf howling in the distance.

Cultural Context:

Many scientists associate societal changes with the cycles of the moon. Studies show that the moon affects tidal movements, which in turn affect people on psychological and sometimes physical levels. Hospital emergency rooms and police departments note a steady rise in accidents, suicides, and crime about the time of a full moon. The words *lunacy* and *lunatic*, in fact, come from the same root as *lunar*.

Because of the moon's association with waxing, waning, and natural cycles such as tides, it has long served as a metaphor for women's bodies and the menstrual cycle. Unfortunately, women themselves have been linked with lunacy in world literature throughout the ages, from Shakespeare's Lady Macbeth to Tennyson's Ophelia to Virginia Woolf herself. Passionate women have been categorized as insane rather than being dealt with directly.

Sandra Gilbert and Susan Gubar's landmark work

of second-wave feminist literary theory, *The Madwoman in the Attic* (1979), discusses this very issue. The title alludes to Bertha Mason, the first wife of Rochester in Charlotte Brontë's *Jane Eyre*, who was locked in the attic for years because presumably she was insane. Gilbert and Gubar argue that Bertha symbolizes the trapped Victorian woman, driven to desperate acts due to a lack of alternatives but not necessarily clinically insane. At the time, it was easier for husbands to place their wives in an asylum or sanitorium and decide that they were ill than to deal with the women's rage and oppression.

Related Superstitions:
Astrological Horoscopes

28. **GARLIC**

General Description:

Scientifically known as Allium sativum, *garlic is part of the onion* (Allium) *family of plants.* Along with its numerous health benefits, garlic is also known for its protective qualities. In particular, garlic is used as a talisman to ward off evil spirits, especially vampires. In the Far East, garlic is also used to restore both physical and psychological health.

Origins:
Grown in the wild in central Asia, garlic has been a cultivated plant since 2000 BCE, when it was grown in

ancient Mesopotamia and Egypt. The Egyptians
believed that garlic's pungent odor imparted strength-
ening powers, so they fed it to their slaves to bolster
the workers' physical ability to build pyramids for the
pharaohs.

In Practice:

In addition to crossing your fingers, making the sign
of the cross, or dabbing yourself with holy water, garlic is a major player in the anti-evil-spirits campaign.
Those who are particularly afraid of vampires are told
to spread garlic on their doorframes and bedposts, to
rub their children's foreheads with cloves of garlic
before bedtime, to wear a wreath of garlic, or to place
a clove within a special locket to ward off these blood-
sucking intruders. In some cultures, to prevent an evil
spirit from entering the body of a recently deceased
person, a piece of garlic is placed in the corpse's mouth.

Aside from its superstitious qualities, garlic is also
beneficial to the human body. A partial list of its uses
and benefits includes helping prevent the onset of
stomach and colon cancer; lowering blood pressure
and cholesterol; preventing blood clots; slowing the
buildup of dangerous plaque in heart arteries; reliev-
ing nasal congestion and head colds; and repelling
insects, especially mosquitoes.

Cultural
Context:

In Bram Stoker's *Dracula* (1897), the most popular
vampire story of all time, Professor Van Helsing uses
garlic to protect Lucy by hanging it in her room and

around her neck. The image has since been re-created in countless books and movies.

Related
Superstitions:

Cross, Evil Eye, Fingers Crossed

---

29. **"GOD BLESS YOU"**

General
Description:

The standard response after one hears a sneeze. For the superstitious, sneezing is good luck, and saying "God bless you" affirms that luck. For less positive (but nonetheless superstitious) people, this utterance ensures that any evil spirits that may have flown out of the body with the sneeze do not return.

Origins:

The particular phrase "God bless you" dates to the onset of the plagues that struck Europe in the sixth century. Sneezing was one of the surest signs that someone had contracted the fatal disease, and when a person began to sneeze uncontrollably, death was imminent. As the epidemic progressed, Pope Gregory the Great passed a law stating that whenever someone sneezed, whoever heard it had to bless that person, praying that his or her life be spared. It is also from this period that covering one's mouth when sneezing became an important practice.

Variations:	Another popular saying related to this involuntary expiration of breath goes: "Sneeze once for a wish, twice for a kiss, three for a letter, or four for something better." Sneezing while talking means that you have just uttered something true, and sneezing simultaneously with others is extremely lucky.
In Practice:	Sneezing has more associated superstitions than perhaps any other bodily function. Upon hearing a person sneeze, the automatic response is "God bless you." All conversation is trumped by the sound of a sneeze, and "God bless you" is a natural interjection, even if the sneezer is a stranger to you. With the blessing, you ensure that whatever malady has befallen that person will be cured. Because the eyes automatically shut when you sneeze, it is also believed that the saying helps shoo away the devil, who may have entered the body when the person was not looking. If you are a Jewish grandmother, you may be inclined to pull the earlobe of the sneezer while also saying "Gesundheit" ("good health"), especially if the sneezer is one of your grandchildren. Alternate right and left ears with each sneeze.
Cultural Context:	Many cultures have similar pronouncements in response to sneezing. The tradition is likely linked to the ancient belief that when a person sneezes, a part of the soul flies away and the heart momentarily stops beating. The blessing for good health, therefore, is

appropriate. The Romans would react to a sneeze by saying, "salve," meaning "good health," and the Greeks wished one another "long life."

Related
Superstitions:

"Bread and Butter," "Break a Leg," "Third Time's a Charm"

30.

GODDESS LAKSHMI

General
Description:

In the Hindu pantheon, the goddess of luck, wealth, wisdom, beauty, and fertility. Lakshmi is pictured as a beautiful woman with four arms, sitting or standing on a lotus flower and often holding a lotus in each hand. She is decorated with gold jewelry and dressed in red clothing. Lakshmi is worshipped by those seeking both material and spiritual success.

Lakshmi's four arms represent *dharma* (righteousness), *kama* (desire), *artha* (wealth), and *moksha* (liberation from the cycle of life and death). In addition to this symbolism, two white elephants are often shown spraying water by Lakshmi's side. Hindus consider the elephant to be holy, and the water spouting from its trunk represents the constant effort one should make to improve one's life. In other words, Lakshmi is not just a goddess who brings luck to those who wish for it, she encourages people to seek out their own successes and maintain a proactive stance.

Origins:	From the Sanskrit word *laksya*, Lakshmi means "aim" or "goal." Also known as Shri, Lakshmi is said to have emerged from the sea of milk, the Hindu version of the primordial waters, holding a red lotus.
In Practice:	Lakshmi is a popular household god, especially among women, and she is worshipped daily. During Diwali (the Hindu festival of lights), however, she receives special status. The custom is to place candles outside your house to receive the blessings of light and wealth from Lakshmi. According to Devdutt Pattanaik, the author of a book about the goddess, for centuries Lakshmi has been invoked with the following prayer:

> *Beautiful goddess seated on a chariot,*
> *Delighted by songs on lustful elephants,*
> *Bedecked with lotuses, pearls, and gems,*
> *Lustrous as fire, radiant as gold,*
> *Resplendent as the sun, calm as the moon,*
> *Mistress of cows and horses—*
> *Take away poverty and misfortune*
> *Bring joy, riches, harvest, and children.*

Cultural Context:	Lakshmi's beauty is so great that all three major Hindu gods—Brahma, Shiva, and Vishnu—desired her as their consort. However, since Brahma had already taken Saraswati and Shiva had married the moon, Lakshmi was given to Vishnu, the god of preservation,

with whom she was reincarnated many times.

Related
Superstitions:

Eight Auspicious Articles, Elephant

31. **GOURD**

General
Description:
☺

The hollowed-out shell of a squash plant. The gourd is used as a bowl, cup, or drum or as a vase or storage unit. It is a symbol of good luck and long life in Taoist and Buddhist cultures.

Origins:

Sau Sing, the god of longevity, carried a walking stick with a gourd attached to the end. Li Tie Guai, the Taoist magician known in mythology as one of the eight immortal beings, carried the elixir of everlasting life in a gourd. From these myths, as well as from the fact that for millennia gourds have been used by travelers to carry and store water and rice, this useful natural container has come to be associated with health and well-being.

Variations:

In feng shui, a vase shaped like a gourd (called a *wo lou*) is used to bring blessings of health and longevity to the home.

In Practice:

A gourd charm will help bring long life to the wearer and aid that person in avoiding accidents and illness.

More practically, gourds can be used for decoration (they are especially popular centerpieces for Thanksgiving and other fall festivals, such as the Jewish holiday of Sukkot), storage, and the service of foods such as dips or side dishes.

Cultural
Context:

The gourd's magical powers have appeared in world literature throughout the ages. The earliest mention may be in the Book of Jonah in the Christian Bible, in which a gourd vine miraculously grows to such proportions that it provides Jonah with much-needed shade. Zora Neale Hurston alluded to this story in her first book, *Jonah's Gourd Vine*, published in 1934. Supernatural gourds figure in folk literature and fairy-tales as well. Gourds have made their way into modern children's books, for example, Baba Wague Diakite's award-winning *The Magic Gourd* (2003).

Related
Superstitions:

Feng Shui

---

32. **GROOMS SEEING BRIDES**

General
Description:

On a wedding day, it is bad luck for the groom to see his fiancée before the ceremony. It is similarly bad luck for the groom to see the wedding dress—whether on the bride or not—before the ceremony.

Origins: This superstitious belief can most likely be traced to the era when arranged marriages were the norm. Because the betrothed had often never met before the wedding day, a less-than-beautiful bride risked being left at the altar if the nervous grooms caught a glimpse of his future wife before making the commitment. The groom might get cold feet—bad luck, indeed.

Today this tradition helps preserve the special moment of the bride's entrance into the wedding hall. If the groom has been kept away from his beloved, he will be all the more enamored upon finally seeing her in her wedding-day finery.

Variations: In traditional Jewish communities, ideally the bride and groom should not see each other during the week before the wedding. First, the separation helps ensure that the inevitable stresses of last-minute wedding preparations will not increase tension between the couple. Second, it gives each partner the opportunity to reflect on the upcoming day and spend some much-needed time alone before embarking on a life together. Third, it ensures that the bride's virginity remains intact. And last, it heightens the joy of the wedding day because (in theory) the bride and groom will be longing to see each other.

In Practice: Even couples who live together before marriage tend to uphold at least some of this tradition, especially since none want to attract bad luck to their imminent union. They may stay with friends or family or in separate hotel rooms the night before the wedding. Seeing each other becomes an issue if the bride and groom wish to take pictures before the ceremony. To accommodate both the tradition and the desire to capture the moment for posterity, some couples organize a private moment to see each other dressed before the wedding and to arrange for photography.

Cultural Context:

In an episode of the sitcom *That '70s Show*, Eric defies the tradition when he finds Donna's wedding dress in her closet. In a daring move he pulls the dress off the hanger, only to hear the horrific sound of material ripping. In a panic, he runs to the kitchen, where he tells his mother what he's done. She offers to sew the tear, so Eric carelessly throws the dress on the table. His mother jumps—"Not on the shoe polish!"—and we see a large black stain on the ripped dress. They then proceed to ruin the dress completely by laundering it in the washing machine. Finally, Eric learns his lesson: It was bad luck indeed to have seen the dress before the big day.

Related Superstitions:

Something Old, Something New, Something Borrowed, Something Blue

GUARDIAN ANGELS

33.

General
Description:

A benevolent heavenly being or supernatural spirit assigned to a specific person or group of persons to provide protection from harm. They form part of the larger group of angels—generally believed to be messengers from God and common to many religions, notably Christianity, Judaism, and Islam. In art, they most often take the form of beautiful, winged humans whose beatific visages impart feelings of calm and security to those they protect. Conversely, they may appear as fierce warriors, complete with armor and weapons at the ready.

Origins:

The idea of angels intervening on behalf of God to help humanity has existed for centuries. Allusions to angels are found in the writings of Greek philosopher Plato, in Babylonian and Assyrian traditions, and in the Old Testament. The individual guardian angel, however, appears in the New Testament (Matthew 18:10), when Jesus proclaims that every child is protected by a single heavenly being. Since then, the notion has been significantly linked with Christianity, although it has been adopted by other religious and secular groups as well. Many people, regardless of religious affiliation, believe that the soul of a departed loved one watches over them as they continue through life.

Variation:
†

Patron saints, a concept related to guardian angels, abound in Christianity, particularly in Catholicism. There is a saint for every day of the week, date, month, event, name, holiday, country, state, river, mountain, fear, love, and hobby. Some of the more popular are St. Patrick, the patron of Ireland, and St. Christopher, the patron of travelers. Lesser known are St. Gertrude of Nivelles, the patron of the fear of mice and rats, and St. Sealtiel, the patron of Thursdays.

In Practice:

Some people believe that their guardian angels are constantly watching over them, protecting their every move. Others feel the need to invoke their guardian angels in times of need, which can be accomplished through meditation, prayer, direct address, or subconsciously, in dreams.

Cultural Context:

The concept of the guardian angel has been portrayed countless times in movies, television shows, and literature. One of the most beloved of all time is Clarence Oddbody, the goofy angel sent to Bedford Falls to save the life of George Bailey, the small-town banker and all-around good guy played by Jimmy Stewart in the 1946 classic film *It's a Wonderful Life*. This movie popularized the belief that an angel gets its wings by saving the life of a deserving human; when the wings are bestowed on the angel, a bell rings. At the end of the movie, when many crises have been averted and

George is joyfully back home, safe and sound, with his wife and children, a bell on the Christmas tree jingles, and George looks up at the ceiling and says, "'Atta boy, Clarence!"

As TV heroes, guardian angels formed the subject of the series *Highway to Heaven* (1984–89), which starred Michael Landon as an angel sent from heaven to help people with their difficulties. A similar plot characterized *Touched by an Angel* (1994–2003), this time starring an eventual quartet of heavenly creatures who come to the aid of those at a crossroads in their lives.

34. **HAMSA**

General Description:

An icon or symbol showing a hand with two short thumblike fingers on either side of three longer fingers and a decoration in the middle (generally an eye figure or a blue stone). The hamsa is used in Middle Eastern countries to ward off the evil eye. It is also known as the hand of Miriam in Jewish contexts and the hand of Fatima in the Muslim tradition.

Origins:

The Arabic word *hamsa* means "five," referring to the five fingers of the hand. Although the exact origins of the hamsa as a talisman are unknown, it is thought that the amulet predates both Islam and Judaism, the two religions most commonly associated with it. In

recent years, it has occasionally been used as a unifying symbol by groups working toward peace in the
Middle East.

One general explanation of the image is that it
represents the protective, open-palmed hand of God.
Another interpretation is that, beyond specific cultural
or religious significance, the "eye and hand" image
represents the complementary acts of seeing and
doing, sensing and acting.

Variations:

The hamsa image and its variants are found in Hindu
and Native American cultures as well as in Tibet. White
Tara, the Buddhist goddess of compassion, is depicted
as having seven eyes: three in her head, two in her
feet, and one in each of the palms of her hands.

In Practice:

Various hamsa amulets are used to protect against the
evil eye. On the streets of Jerusalem and in the open
markets of Istanbul, for example, merchants sell hamsas
made of different types of metal (gold, silver) or synthetic materials (plastics), sometimes with gemstones
inserted into them. Hamsas are hung in places of
business and homes for protection, and they are sometimes incorporated with other good-luck images; for
example, inscribed on the palm may be a fish, Star of
David, or a Hebrew prayer for peace in the home or
success in business. Hamsas with the prayer for travelers
make popular key chains, and the amulets are also used
in wind chimes and mobiles for babies' cribs.

| Cultural Context: | Variations of the hamsa theme of eyes and hands appear on the 1979 cover of Stephen King's book *Night Shift* and, more recently, as the horrific character called The Pale Man from Guillermo del Toro's award-winning 2006 movie *Pan's Labyrinth*. |

Related Superstitions:

Blue, Evil Eye, Fish, Nazar Boncugu

HEATHER

General Description:

:)

A small shrub (Calluna vulgaris)*, native to Europe and Asia Minor, that grows especially well in heath and moorland climates from late June to November.* The plant's blossoms, particularly the white ones, are a prominent good-luck charm in Scotland, where the flower is synonymous with Scottish culture and folklore, much like the four-leaf clover in Ireland. Because white heather is rarer than the purple type, it is considered lucky to stumble upon such a blossom in nature.

Origins:

Several theories exist to explain why heather became a lucky symbol in Scotland. One is that white heather grows only in places on a battlefield that have been untouched by death; another is that it grows at locations where faerie beings die. Among the most poignant and popular traditions is found in the folktale of Malvina, daughter of the Celtic bard named

Ossian. Malvina's fiancé, Oscar, was killed in battle. When a messenger arrived to tell of her lover's death, he brought with him a sprig of purple heather over which the dying Oscar had spoken his last words of devotion to his beloved. Distraught, Malvina ran into the fields and sobbed. When her tears turned the purple flowers white, she declared that, from then on, white heather would bring only good luck to those who found it, banishing the bad luck that the purple flower had come to symbolize for her.

In Practice: Because of the history of white heather—Malvina's tragic love story and her selfless wish for others to be happier—the flower now plays a prominent part in Scottish weddings. Scottish brides and grooms incorporate the plant into their wedding ensemble, with the men wearing a sprig in their lapels and the bridesmaids carrying some in their bouquets or hair. Brides tend to carry a lucky horseshoe decorated with fresh heather as they walk down the aisle, instead of or in addition to a traditional floral bouquet.

Cultural Context:

Before the discovery of hops, heather was used to brew beer in the Middle Ages. It is also the national flower of Norway. In England, heather was a dominant literary symbol in nineteenth-century novels. In Emily Brontë's classic book *Wuthering Heights* (1847), the stormy relationship between Catherine and Heathcliff takes place against the backdrop of the craggy moors dotted with heather. When the famous film version of the novel was made in 1939, real heather was imported from England to give the California stage setting a more authentic look.

Related Superstitions:

Four-Leaf Clover, Horseshoe

35. 📷 **HENNA**

General Description: 🙂

A natural red-orange dye made from leaves of the henna plant (Lawsonia inermis). It is used to paint temporary tattoos on hands, feet, and other body parts as well as to dye hair and nails; it is also used to tint animal hides and textiles. Common for centuries throughout India, North Africa, and the Middle East, henna application has recently become widespread throughout the rest of the world. Henna designs bring good luck to those who are painted. They are used to enhance happiness and fertility and to avert the evil eye.

Origins:

Ancient references to the art of body painting using henna are found in both India and Egypt. Achaeologists have discovered five-thousand-year-old mummies from ancient Egypt whose fingers and fingernails had been dyed with henna. Indian murals dating to the fourth or fifth century depict images of henna-painted goddesses.

The global popularity of the tradition and the competing regional histories make the origins of henna something of a mystery, although it seems clear that the art form has no single source. One explanation states that in ancient India, the henna plant was discovered to have cooling properties. In the sometimes unbearably hot climate, Indians would prepare a mud mixture infused with henna leaves and dip their hands and feet in it. Even after the mud dried and fell off, the henna stain remaining on the skin would help cool the body temperature. In time, women grew to dislike the splotchy look of dipped appendages and began painting a single dot on their palms instead. That single mark developed into patterns that became increasingly elaborate, eventually evolving into the art form we know today.

In Practice: The most common practice involving henna is the art of mehndi, a form of temporary skin decoration that is popular in Arabic and Southeast Asian cultures. It is especially well known as a decoration on Indian brides and is applied during elaborate prewedding ceremonies.

Henna is most commonly applied on the hands and feet. Artists use a variety of techniques and instruments, applying the henna paste with brushes, bottles, or conelike applicators. During application, the most important requirement is patience. Elaborate designs can take several hours to create, and the person being painted must remain as still as possible. The paste can then take several hours to dry.

Although these designs are called tattoos, they do not involve needles and are completely painless and temporary. A typical henna application lasts between a few days and a few weeks, depending on where it is placed and how often the person bathes or sweats.

Arabic henna artists favor floral designs; Indians tend toward finer, lacy patterns. In African countries, designs are generally larger and more geometric. Hennas are most commonly drawn to commemorate special occasions, namely engagements, weddings, the eighth month of pregnancy, childbirth, circumcision, and religious holidays and celebrations.

In addition, henna is used as a natural red hair dye, often favored over chemical alternatives.

Cultural Context:

♫

Henna tattoos can be purchased at street festivals and carnivals worldwide. They are now a popular feature at so-called Bollywood parties, a trend of Indian pop-culture-themed get-togethers. Many entertainers and actors, including Prince, Gwen Stefani, Demi Moore, and Mia Sorvino, have been spotted sporting henna tattoos. Madonna has been especially fond of henna art, featuring a hand tattoo of the "Om" symbol in her music video "Frozen."

Related Superstitions:

Evil Eye

36. 🔘 **HORSESHOE**

General
Description:
🙂

A protective covering for the hoof originally made of iron but now often made of steel, plastics, and other materials. Glued or nailed onto the hooves of a horse, horseshoes safeguard the feet of domesticated, draught, and racing horses from wear by elements such as cement or cobblestone. When horseshoes fall off (and they often do), they become endowed with lucky energies that will transfer to the finder.

Origins:

Several existing theories explain the origins of the horseshoe as a good-luck symbol. One dates to the tenth century, when the Archbishop of Canterbury, a trained blacksmith, nailed a horseshoe to the hoof of the Devil, who came to him in disguise. When Satan realized that the shoe caused him pain, the archbishop offered to remove it, but only if Satan agreed to avoid homes with horseshoes hung over the doors. He agreed. As a result, those seeking to avoid run-ins with evil decorate with this U-shaped charm.

Blacksmiths, even those who don't serve illustrious clients such as Satan, were generally revered artisans and were believed to have magical powers because they worked with fire and iron (both supernatural, alchemical elements). Furthermore, the original iron horseshoes were held in place with seven iron nails, a number that is particularly auspicious. The association with good luck is further strengthened by the

Icon Key

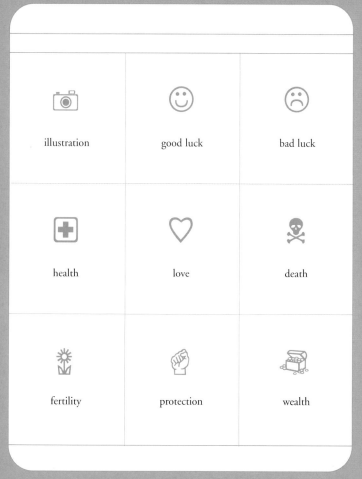

illustration

good luck

bad luck

health

love

death

fertility

protection

wealth

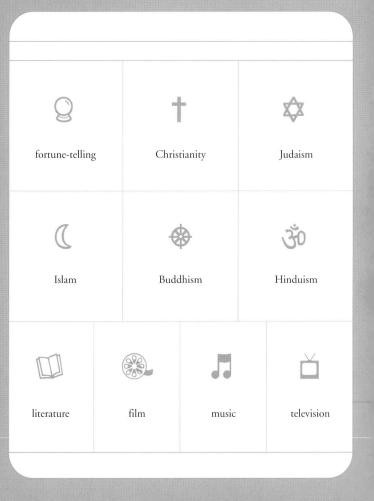

fortune-telling

Christianity

Judaism

Islam

Buddhism

Hinduism

literature

film

music

television

Color Plates

1. **acorn**

2. **akuaba**

3. **aladdin's lamp**

4. **astrological horoscope**

5. **black cat**

6. **bread and butter**

7. broken mirror

8. carrying a bride over a threshold

9. **chai (18)**

10. **charm bracelet**

11. **chinese astrology**

12. **coming and going**

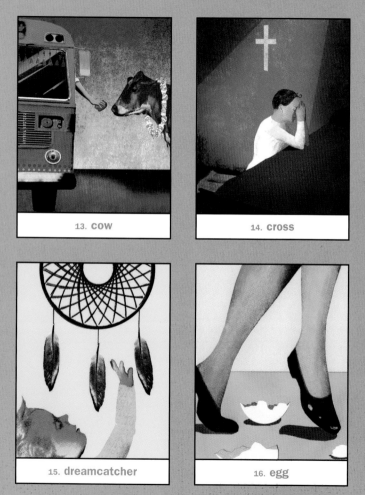

13. **cow**

14. **cross**

15. **dreamcatcher**

16. **egg**

17. **eight auspicious articles**

18. **elephant**

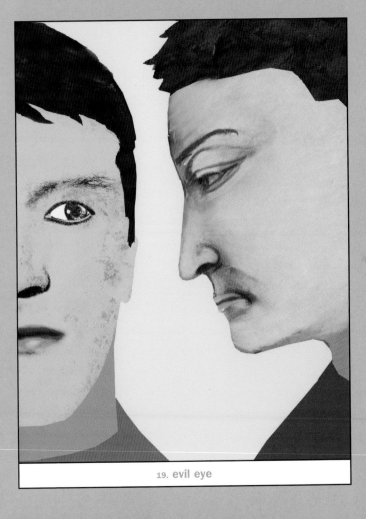

19. **evil eye**

20. fates

21. **fingers crossed**

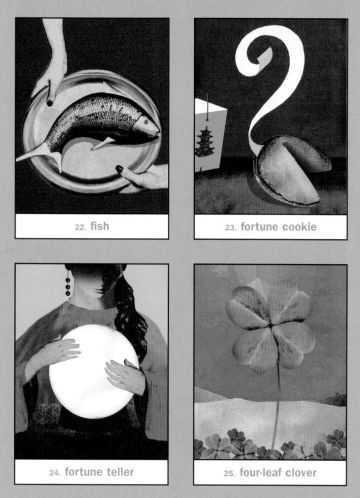

22. **fish**

23. **fortune cookie**

24. **fortune teller**

25. **four-leaf clover**

26. **frog**

27. **full moon**

28. **garlic**

29. **"god bless you"**

30. **goddess lakshmi**

31. **gourd**

32. grooms seeing brides

33. **guardian angels**

34. **hamsa**

35. **henna**

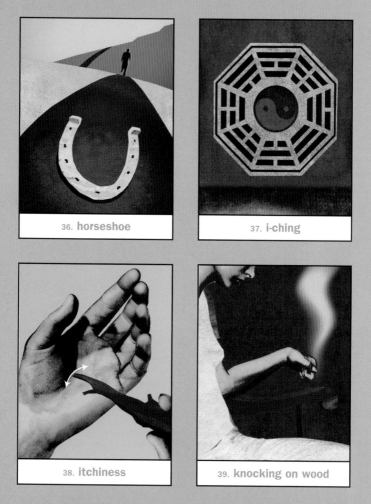

36. **horseshoe**

37. **i-ching**

38. **itchiness**

39. **knocking on wood**

40. **ladybug**

41. **lady luck**

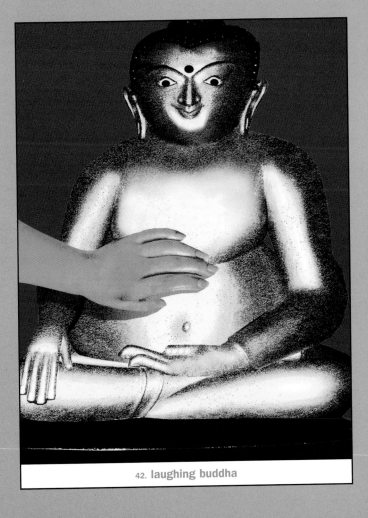

42. laughing buddha

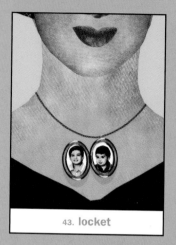

43. **locket**

44. **lucky number 7**

45. **lucky penny**

46. **making a wish**

47. maneki neko

48. **mantra**

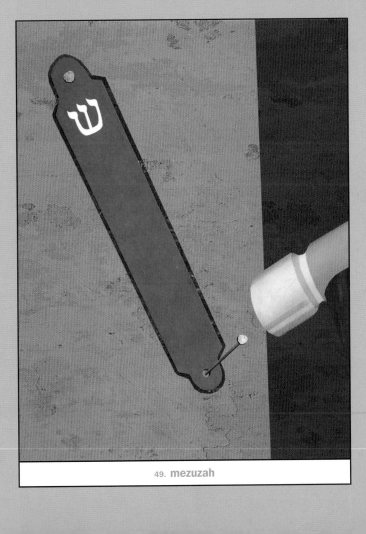

49. **mezuzah**

50. **nazar boncugu (evil eye bead)**

51. nine lives of cats

52. **opening an umbrella inside**

53. **ouija board**

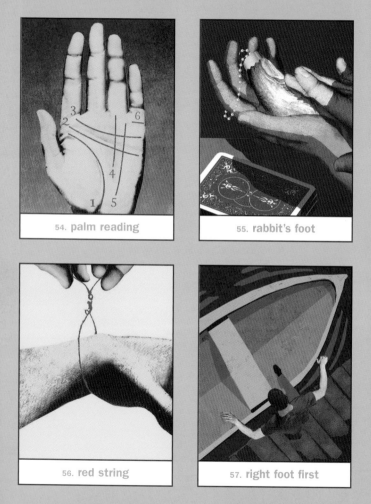

54. **palm reading**

55. **rabbit's foot**

56. **red string**

57. **right foot first**

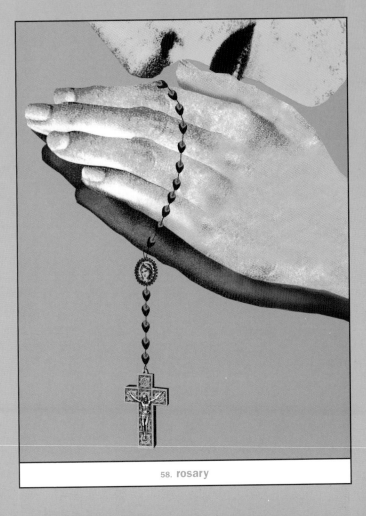

58. **rosary**

59. runes

60. **scarab**

61. **shooting star**

62. **salt**

63. **talisman**

64. **tarot cards**

65. **unicorn**

66. **unlucky number 13**

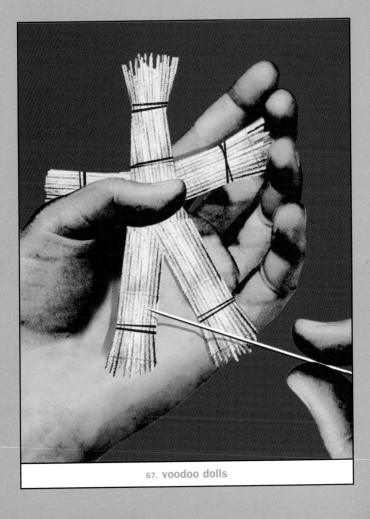

67. **voodoo dolls**

68. **walking under a ladder**

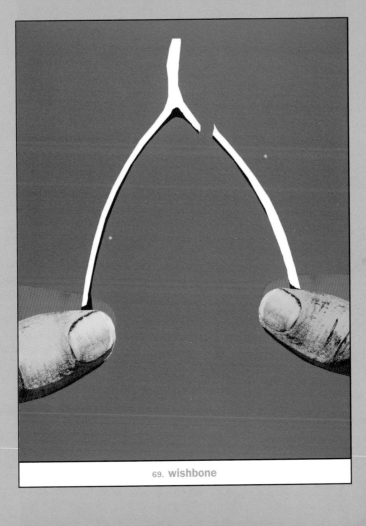

69. **wishbone**

70. **wishing well**

horseshoe's crescent shape, since the moon has long been a symbol of fertility and higher powers.

Variations: We all know that witches travel on broomsticks, pitchforks, or the occasional owl. Why? Because witches are afraid of horses. For this reason, horseshoes can also be used to ward off a bad witch, as can a horse with a braided tail.

In Practice: The person who finds a castoff horseshoe should bring it home and hang it over a doorframe to promote positive energy, health, and fertility and to guard against evil spirits. A universally popular good-luck symbol, the horseshoe is especially coveted if found on a road, with the open end pointing toward you. It may also be carried as a charm. Several cultures disagree whether the horseshoe should be hung with the points facing up or down. Some believe that a horseshoe hanging with the points facing up will help the good luck remain enclosed within; by contrast, those who prefer the facedown position believe it to be the only way for the good luck to float down to the recipient. Still others find a middle ground by hanging their horseshoe on a hinge that allows them to shift it up or down. That way, the horseshoe can fill up with good luck and then shower its beneficence down into the house.

Although the ideal is to find an actual used horseshoe abandoned on a horse-traveled road, a plethora of mass-produced charms are available for those unfortunate not to stumble upon them by chance. Gamblers—particularly those who bet on races—are especially fond of the horseshoe charm.

In Mexico, a horseshoe is sold as part of an elaborate good-luck package possessing anti-evil properties. Red thread is wound around the horseshoe, which is then decorated with crosses, images of saints, sequins, and glitter. The whole is wrapped in clear vinyl. While the horseshoe may not be easily recognizable enveloped in this shiny package, it serves as the crucial luck-bringing foundation.

Cultural Context:

In fourteenth-century England, soldiers enjoyed playing a game called quoits (a version of an earlier game popular with ancient Roman soldiers), in which a metal ring was tossed toward a stake set in the ground. The goal was to land the ring around the stake. This game evolved into horseshoes, once a backyard pastime and now a full-fledged sport, complete with a world championship competition. It is played as follows: Two to four people pitch horseshoes at a stake set into the ground at a specific distance from the players and within two rectangular areas. If one of the horseshoes successfully rings the stake (called a "ringer"), the thrower receives three points. Fewer points are awarded for horseshoes that land close to the stake, and fewer still for those that land in the outer perimeters of the rectangle. The first player to reach twenty-one points wins.

Related
Superstitions: Charm Bracelet, Evil Eye, Heather, Lucky Numbers

37.   **I CHING**

General
Description: *An ancient Chinese oracle text used to apply order to
seemingly random events.* The *I Ching* is also known as
the *Book of Changes*; variant spellings include *I Jing*
and *Yi Jing*. It contains three-line diagrams called tri-
grams that correspond to the powers of nature (later
multiplied into 64 hexagrams) and explains how to
use these symbols to interpret the future and acquire
wisdom.

Origins: According to legend, the *I Ching* dates to the time of
a mythical emperor named Fu Xi, who ruled China in
the mid-2800s BCE. However, it is most associated
with Confucius (ca. 551–479 BCE), who wrote the
book of commentary explaining the significance of
the various hexagrams. This commentary, when combined with the study of Chinese astrology and the five
elements (earth, fire, metal, water, and wood), came
to be known as the *I Ching*.

Variations: The *I Ching* is more than just a personal oracle. It is
used in conjunction with feng shui to map out space
and analyze energies. The *bagua*, an octagonal diagram containing the symbols of the *I Ching* (which,

in turn, relate to various aspects of life experience and human nature), is mapped onto a specific space. Each of the eight directions (north, south, east, west, northeast, northwest, southeast, and southwest) has specific associations with the five elements and with various patterns and principles of life. By interpreting the energy of the bagua, the *I Ching* informs the optimum feng shui for a space.

In Practice: As with many other aspects of Chinese philosophy, much of the *I Ching* reflects the dualistic principles of yin and yang. Yin is the feminine, passive energy associated with divided lines. Yang is the masculine, active energy associated with undivided lines.

When you pose questions to the *I Ching*, you cast a series of coins or yarrow stalks and then convert the patterns of those cast objects into the form of a hexagram. Each hexagram conveys a unique message, and you should be able to infer the answer to your question by interpreting that message. (Note that the process of casting with yarrow stalks is more complicated; if you are a beginner, it's best to use the coins.)

Each side of the coin (heads or tails) is assigned to represent either yin or yang. Yin carries a value of three, and yang a value of two. After asking a question of the oracle, cast the three coins six times, each time noting the value of the coins as they land. Next, draw lines corresponding to those six numbers, resulting in a six-line diagram called a hexagram. There are sixty-four potential hexagrammic configurations, and each has a specific reading. Look up the hexagram in the oracle book to find the answer to your specific question.

As with any ancient tradition, the *I Ching* can be difficult to understand. The text is centuries old, and, for the uninitiated, the process of finding your hexagram can be equally confusing. Although watered-down, popular-culture versions do exist (see "Cultural Context"), be wary of the easier road. The path to understanding and revelation through the *I Ching* is meant to be a long one, filled with enlightenment that can come only with trial and error. Only by struggling with the material will you find true meaning.

Cultural Context: The *I Ching* has been translated into dozens of languages and is also available online. In addition, Web sites will cast yarrow stalks for you at random, as in a lottery drawing, and provide your reading instantaneously.

Related Superstitions: Chinese Astrology, Feng Shui

38. **ITCHINESS**

General Description: *The sensation or discomfort that causes an urge to scratch.*

Origins: Several superstitious beliefs are linked to itchiness—
            itchy noses, hands, ears, feet, head, and elbows. Each
            type is accompanied by an attendant signification,
            ranging from meeting the love of your life to knowing
            when someone is speaking ill of you. These supersti-
            tions are sometimes linked with the Celtic tradition
            of touching wood to bring about good fortune (see
            "Knocking on Wood," page 133). Because of this
            association, touching wood with an itchy hand is
            believed to ensure the good luck it foretells.

In Practice: Be prepared! The myriad itches and the luck they
            bring are difficult to keep straight. When the outside
            of your nose itches, you will soon be kissed. When
            the inside of your nose itches, you are about to run
            into some bad luck. When your hand itches, particu-
            larly the palm, it means that you'll be coming into
            money. If you are a stickler, the left palm itch indi-
            cates coming money, and the itching of the right
            palm might mean that you are going to lose money.
            When the left palm itches, it is advisable to scratch it
            with a piece of wood to make sure you do indeed
            receive the money that's coming to you. If you experi-
            ence itching in your right palm, it is best not to
            scratch it at all. When your right ear itches, someone
            is speaking well of you. When your left ear itches,
            someone is speaking ill of you. When your feet itch,
            you will soon go on a journey; when your head itches,
            you'll be coming into luck. And finally, when your

elbow itches, you have a new love on the horizon.

Cultural
Context:

One itch that is best to avoid is the seven-year itch, made famous by the 1955 movie of the same name and starring Marilyn Monroe. In popular parlance, a seven-year itch is the urge to try something new, particularly in relationships (for example, on your seventh wedding anniversary, you may start looking for blonde neighbors in white dresses with whom to consider having an affair while your wife and child are away in Maine for the summer). For the good of your family, it is best not to scratch this particular itch.

Related
Superstitions:

Knocking on Wood

JADE

General
Description:

A green (or sometimes white) gemstone most famous in China but popular worldwide. It is carried for good luck, good health, and to ward off evil spirits.

Origins:

Of the two varieties of jade, jadeite and nephrite, the latter has been used in China for more than four thousand years. A symbol of wealth and power, jade was called *yu*, the "royal gem." As ancient Chinese kingdoms fought among themselves, their jade emblems were often caught in the crossfire, stolen and repossessed by rivals. Because kings placed such high value on jade objects, the gem was thought to have noble qualities and supernatural powers. It was also used to decorate the tombs of aristocrats.

Jade is also extremely strong and durable and consequently was used during the Stone Age to fashion knives and other weapons. It was associated with heaven and earth because it was found in either mountains or riverbeds, lending it an aura of power.

In Practice: Although not as expensive as other jewels such as diamonds or rubies, true jade is quite valuable, and objects made from it should be handled carefully. American collectors tend to favor clear, bright, emerald-green jade, whereas in China the most valuable stones are milky, light green ones. Chinese tradition holds that as the jade brings you good luck, it darkens in color (therefore, lighter jade has more luck to impart). Whatever your preference, jade is used to make all types of decorative objects, jewelry, and charms.

Cultural   As one of the seven wonders of the world, the Taj
Context: Mahal in India is one of the most beautiful buildings ever constructed. Built over the course of two decades by more than twenty thousand workers, it was commissioned by the seventeenth-century emperor Shah Jahan in memory of his wife, Mumtaz Mahal, who died in childbirth at age thirty-nine. Among other

materials imported from around the world, jade from China is used throughout the impressive structure.

Related
Superstitions:

Amber, Charm Bracelet

KARMA

General
Description:
☺ ☹

From the Sanskrit word for "action" or "deed," karma is the idea that a person's circumstances, in every incarnation, are determined by actions in past and current lives. Within a single life span, doing good deeds will bring you equal measure of good fortune; if you perform bad deeds, expect bad things in return. As opposed to the concept of destiny, in which all things are preordained, karma presupposes that everything happens for a reason and that we are each responsible for determining those reasons.

Origins:
卐 ॐ

The cycle of cause and effect and human responsibility is especially prominent in Buddhist and Hindu religious traditions. Notably, karma is introduced in the third conversation between Krishna and Arjuna, as related in the Hindu text called the *Bhagavad Gita*. In that exchange, Arjuna grapples with the question of whether action or wisdom is more essential and considers the inevitable human desire to sin. Krishna explains the notion of karma: the importance of our actions in this world and their intentions, as they relate to past, present, and future incarnations.

Variations:

In general parlance, karma is ofen used synonymously with aura, as in "She has good karma" or "This house has bad karma." Although it does not correspond with the term's original meaning, this use is popular and widespread.

In Practice:

Because the main goal of karma is to serve others selflessly as a path to enlightenment and spiritual growth, it is important to do something that is personally meaningful, for example, using a particular skill or talent to help others, joining a volunteer association, or simply performing random acts of kindness. The idea is that by performing such kind, selfless acts as though they were inevitable, you come one step closer to God as well as to the enlightenment that follows you through this life and into the next incarnation.

Cultural Context:

Karma yoga is the practice of minimizing your ego so that you can act selflessly, without attachment to the perceived consequences of your actions. According to the *Bhagavad Gita*, the principal goal of karma yoga is to attain union through action—to influence the world by first becoming in tune with yourself. Although Westerners think of yoga as a form of physical exercise, in its original context yoga is a path of life, a way of thinking about the world. The physical movements are only one part of this overarching philosophical system. Karma yoga is no exception. Although today karma yoga is taught in the context of physical yoga—stretching and bending in ways that aid meditative and personal growth—it is mainly concerned with the performance of good deeds, such as donating money to charities and spending time volunteering for worthy causes. In this way, you influence not only the karma you send into your next incarnation but also the energies of the world at large in this, your current incarnation.

Related
Superstitions: Destiny, Fates

39. KNOCKING ON WOOD

General
Description: *The act of knocking on, or touching, wood, is performed*
                 to ward off evil spirits or bring about good luck.

Variant: Simply saying "knock on wood" is thought to suffice, although the physical act is always preferred.

Origins: Although this superstition is usually linked to Christianity—the wood in question refers to that of the crucifix on which Jesus Chist died—the act of knocking on wood dates back farther in the annals of human history. In ancient times, pagan peoples believed that spirits lived in trees. For that reason, knocking on or touching trees invoked the help of these good spirits and awakened them to come to your aid.

In Practice: In hopes of bringing about a favorable outcome, one might say the following: "I should be getting my promotion any day now . . . knock on wood!" In another context, you may want to touch wood when you mention something like your amazing track record of having zero parking tickets. The belief is that, if you don't touch wood, you might jinx yourself into getting a ticket.

Cultural Context: You may be most familiar with this phrase not because of what it signifies, but because of Eddie Floyd's 1966 hit song "Knock on Wood," which includes the onomatopoeic sound in the chorus. The tune became so popular that even its cover versions—notably Amii Stewart's 1979 Grammy-nominated rendition—became number-one hits.

Related Superstitions: Cross

40. 📷 **LADYBUG**

Other Names: Ladybird, lady beetle.

General
Description:
    A female beetle of the family Coccinellidae. It measures between 0.04 and 0.4 inches long (1–10 mm) and has red, orange, or yellow wing covers that are often spotted with black dots.

Origins:
✝
    The idea that female beetles are lucky and the origin of their popular name date to the Middle Ages. When aphids threatened to destroy crops, devout farmers desperately called to the Virgin Mary for help. She answered by sending a host of beetles, which ate the offending bugs and saved the crops. In thanks, the farmers named ladybugs after Mary, whom Chistians call "Our Lady," and declared them worthy of protection.

In Practice:
☺ ☹
    Having a ladybug land on you, or even seeing one, is good luck. Consequently, killing one will certainly bring bad luck. To determine the type of good fortune the ladybug will bring, it is common practice to count the spots on the wing covers. If there are fewer than seven spots, the insect will bring a good harvest; if there are more than seven, a famine. The number of spots can also correspond to the number of months in which you will have good luck after finding the ladybug; some believe it may indicate the number of children a woman will bear. If a ladybug lands on the

hand of a single woman, she will soon be married, and if one is found in your house during wintertime, the season will be a good one. Finally, never kill a ladybug. When you are done watching it crawl around on your body, simply release the insect out-doors, gently blowing on it until it takes flight. When it does, be sure to make a wish.

Cultural Context:

The story of ladybug saviors in the Middle Ages has a modern counterpart. In the late 1880s, scale insects threatened to decimate citrus groves in California, so, in desperation, the state's farmers imported thousands of Australian ladybugs. Within two years, the scale insects had vanished and the trees began to bear fruit again. The little red bugs had saved a multimillion-dollar industry.

Related Superstitions:

Amber, Jade, Scarab, Wishbone

41. 📷 **LADY LUCK**

General Description: 😊

The personification of luck as a woman, used especially in the context of gambling. She is invoked to bring good fortune rather than bad.

Origins:

The notion of Lady Luck refers to Fortuna (known in Greece as Tyche), the ancient Roman goddess of fertility, fate, chance, and, of course, fortune. Fortuna is often pictured next to a wheel, known as the Wheel of Fortune, which she spins to determine the details of humans' lives.

In Practice: At casinos, many male gamblers have a penchant for asking attractive women to blow on their dice before casting them. The hope is that the woman will serve as their Lady Luck. Note that if a woman has accompanied a man to the casino, it is considered inappropriate for her to blow on another man's dice.

Cultural Context: Lady Luck features prominently in the song "Luck Be a Lady Tonight," from the musical *Guys and Dolls*. The song tells the story of gambler Sky Masterson, who hopes to win a bet that will determine whether or not he can save his romantic relationship. The tune went on to become one of Frank Sinatra's biggest hits.

Related Superstitions: Beginner's Luck

42. **LAUGHING BUDDHA**

General Description: *A popular Buddhist icon known as* Hotei *in Japan or* Pu-Tai *in China, the Laughing Buddha is one of seven lucky gods.* He is pictured with a large, naked belly, a smiling countenance, and a cloth sack and is often depicted with children at his feet.

Origins: Pu-Tai was a legendary Zen monk from China who
           lived during the Liang Dynasty, more than one thou-
           sand years ago. Pu-Tai wandered from place to place
           with a cloth sack that contained food, sweets for chil-
           dren, and the woes of the world, which he took from
           people and placed in his bag, believing that to achieve
           enlightenment he first had to help others. Known for
           his kindness to the poor and to children, Pu-Tai was
           thought to be an incarnation of the future Buddha.
           The Laughing Buddha embodies Pu-Tai's best quali-
           ties, including his large belly, that symbolize happi-
           ness and prosperity.

           Another possible model for the Laughing
           Buddha is Angida, a monk who was famous for his
           ability to catch snakes and rid them of their venom
           before they had a chance to bite passers-by. Angida
           also carried a sack, in which he put the snakes.
           Similarly, his kindness and selflessness lead to
           enlightenment.

In Practice: It is thought that rubbing the Laughing Buddha's
   😊   belly will bring good luck. Facing the statue, think of
               the woe and sadness you would like to be rid of and
               of the happiness you'd like to replace it with. By rub-
               bing the Buddha's tummy, he will gather up your sad-
               ness and put it in his sack. In return, you will discover
               that a good life is attainable in this incarnation, thus
               allowing you to find your path to fulfillment.

Cultural Context:
Want to do more than rub the Buddha's belly? You can eat him for about $30 (plus shipping, handling, and gift wrap) if you order a chocolate version from the online purveyor chocolatedeities.com. The New York specialists believe that molding deities out of cocoa, which the Aztecs called the "food of the gods," helps lighten the religious experience. Thanks to this edible version, you can fill yourself with the Laughing Buddha's positive energy or pass him along to a friend in need of good luck.

Related Superstitions:
Aladdin's Lamp, Eight Auspicious Articles

43. LOCKET

General Description:
An ornamental pendant, usually worn on a necklace, that opens to reveal a photograph or keepsake object such as a trinket or a lock of hair. Lucky charms are often placed in lockets, enabling the wearer to carry them discreetly everywhere they are needed.

Origins:
Like many objects of adornment, lockets have existed for centuries. In the 1700s, lockets contained painted images of loved ones, a tradition that evolved into photographs as technology developed. Along with charm bracelets, lockets became highly fashionable in England during the reign of Queen Victoria

(1837–1901) and appear frequently in antique jewelry collections of that period.

In Practice: The quintessential object of sentimental value, the locket is usually worn by women, who may receive them as gifts on Valentine's Day, Mother's Day, or other special occasions. The most popular objects to place inside a locket are pictures of family members, especially children, husbands, or parents. Another common item often tucked into the charm is a lock of hair from a loved one, perhaps a deceased relative or a solider away at war. By holding symbols of loved ones close to the heart, the wearer sends positive energy to those being remembered and wishes them luck.

Cultural Context: One of the quirkiest locket objects forms a storyline in Mel Brooks's 1993 spoof film titled *Robin Hood: Men in Tights*. Robin Hood must unlock Maid Marion's chastity belt with a key that is held in a locket. Unfortunately—and in true Mel Brooks's fashion—the key doesn't turn. Marion's suggestion? "Call the locksmith!"

Related Superstitions: Charm Bracelet

LUCK OF THE IRISH

General
Description:

☺ ☹

An expression used in various contexts, usually around St. Patrick's Day, to describe aspects of Irish life and culture. Whether or not the phrase is sarcastic (in other words, whether it relates to good or bad luck) is debatable and usually depends on context.

Origins:

The American traditions of St. Patrick's Day parades, corned beef and cabbage, green beer, green clothes, and all types of revelry in the name of the "luck of the Irish" are just that—American traditions. In Ireland, St. Patrick's Day was originally a religious holiday; pubs were closed and people went to church.

In fact, the phrase "luck of the Irish" was mainly used sarcastically to explain the many hardships the Irish people have faced over their long and complicated history. Murphy's Law (the notion that whatever can go wrong, will go wrong) is distinctly Irish. All bad occurrences and events—such as potato famine, civil war, religious instability, alcoholism, and mass emigration—were chalked up to the unfortunate "luck of the Irish." When good luck did occur (such as when a group of Irish men hit it big in the silver and gold rushes of the nineteenth century), the phrase was used in a tongue-in-cheek manner to mean "dumb luck" rather than true good luck.

Variations: Lucky Irish leprechauns, as they appear on St.
                  Patrick's Day cards and Saturday morning cartoons,
                  are not in keeping with the original descriptions of
                  the little green men. According to Irish folklore, lep-
                  rechauns were stingy, grouchy creatures who made
                  shoes for fairies and were generally not cute or cuddly,
                  much less lucky.

In Practice: To obtain the good luck of the Irish, try kissing the
                  Blarney Stone (an actual stone set into a wall at
                  Blarney Castle in southern Ireland). Other options
                  include discovering a four-leaf clover or a leprechaun
                  (with, of course, his pot of gold at the end of the
                  rainbow).

Cultural   Frank McCourt, the author of the best-selling mem-
Context: oir *Angela's Ashes*, would be hard pressed to say that
                  the Irish were an inherently lucky people. After being
                  raised in unspeakable poverty with an abusive, alco-
                  holic father and experiencing the death of young sib-
                  lings, illness, and crime, nineteen-year-old McCourt
                  immigrated to the United States. In America, he
                  found work, was drafted into the army, and then pur-
                  sued a college degree, thanks to the G.I. Bill. After
                  teaching creative writing in the New York public
                  school system for twenty-seven years, McCourt retired
                  and wrote his memoir. Upon being published in
                  1996, the book won a Pulitzer Prize and a National
                  Book Award. It held a place on the *New York Times*

best-seller list for hundreds of weeks, sold millions of copies, has been translated into more than twenty-five languages, and spawned two sequels and a major motion picture. Although McCourt's early life was certainly difficult, his successes and triumphs over great odds are the best of what we might call the luck o' the Irish.

Related Superstitions:

Four-Leaf Clover

44. 📷 **LUCKY NUMBER 7**

General Description:

🙂

The digit that comes between 6 and 8. Certain numbers are believed to be inherently lucky, making them sought after on many levels. The most famous and oft-cited lucky number is 7, although 3 holds a close second because of the well-known phrase "third time's a charm."

Origins:

For millennia, lucky numbers and numerology systems have been a part of nearly every culture. From Pythagoras in ancient Greece to Christian mystics to Jewish Kabbalists and their system of Gematria (in which letters are given numerical values) to the Hindu vedas, people have always looked for the deeper meaning of mathematics as well as of numbers themselves. Numbers typically associated with luck in Western cultures, such as 1, 3, 7, 9, and 13, share certain mathematical similarities with prime numbers (which are evenly divisible only by 1 and the number itself).

Seven in particular has long been associated with luck. There are seven days in a week, and God rested on the seventh day of creation (also known as the Sabbath, a word related to *sabbatical*, in which the seventh year is taken off). There are seven sacraments in the Roman Catholic Church as well as seven virtues to offset the seven deadly sins. There are seven wonders of the world and seven seas. In Japan, there are seven lucky gods, and in ancient Babylonia, there were believed to be seven holy planets in the universe.

Variations: In China, even numbers trump odd ones, in terms of luck. Because good things come in pairs (such as couples), the Chinese traditionally present gifts in even numbers, especially at weddings. This practice helps explain why, in China, 8 is luckier than 7. Chinese people will pay top dollar to have eights in their bank account numbers or on license plates since that digit is associated with money. The word for "eight" in Chinese sounds like "ba," which means "wealth" or "fortune."

In Practice: In both Jewish and Hindu weddings, the number 7 features prominently. At a Jewish wedding, the bride circles the groom seven times at the beginning of the ceremony to symbolize the building of their new home together and the opening of the seven gates of heaven; the act also serves to remind them that they will now be together every day of the week. During the ceremony, the betrothed are given the seven blessings of marriage. At a Hindu wedding celebration, the bride and groom circle a ceremonial fire four times and conclude the wedding by taking seven steps together as they recite the seven vows of marriage.

Cultural Context:

The most popular wedding day in recent memory was the auspicious date of July 7, 2007 (or 7/7/07). Thousands of couples booked venues years in advance, and hundreds of thousands more were turned away because they did not act fast enough. Hotels, caterers, photographers, and wedding planners were the most highly sought-after professionals that summer and were often paid double or triple their usual fees by couples convinced that they had to have this lucky day as an anniversary. In addition, gamblers made sure to book rooms in Las Vegas months in advance, and the casinos enjoyed unprecedented numbers of patrons during the weekend of July 7, 2007.

Related Superstitions:

Chai, Destiny Number, Master Numbers, "Third Time's a Charm," Unlucky Number 13

45. 📷 **LUCKY PENNY**

General
Description:

A low-denomination unit of currency in several English-speaking countries, including the United Kingdom, the United States, Canada, and Australia. Variations of the word *penny* and its use as a coin include *pfennig* (Germany) and *penni* (Finland).

Origins:

The original link between pennies and luck is unclear, but the coin has become associated with the famous folk rhyme "Find a penny, pick it up / All day long you'll have good luck."

In Practice:
☺ ☹

One of the most popular and widespread symbols of good luck, finding a penny whose "heads" (the side bearing a figural likeness) faces up is thought to bring good luck. If the "tails" side is faceup, leave the coin where you found it—bottoms-up pennies tend to bring bad luck.

Once the lucky penny is firmly in your possession, there are many ways to use it to your advantage. Toss it into a wishing well or other body of water while making a wish; put it in your purse or wallet to attract wealth; or attach it to a bride's shoe on her wedding day to attract good fortune to her marriage. Some people treasure pennies found on special days or in favorite places, carrying them for years, or at least on important occasions. For many, however, the most practical use for a lucky penny is to scratch away the film covering the prizes printed on a lottery card.

Cultural Context:	According to the U.S. Mint, only forty known copper-alloy 1943 pennies were ever created. Because at that time copper and nickel were reserved for much-needed war supplies, almost all pennies minted that year were made of zinc-coated steel. The few copper-alloy examples were produced accidentally at the start of the steel penny pressing. In 1958 one of these rare pennies sold for $40,000; in 1996 another garnered more than $80,000. If you happen to find one of the collectible coins, you are well advised to pick it up straightaway, regardless of whether it's heads or tails side up!
Related Superstitions:	Making a Wish, Something Old, Something New

46. MAKING A WISH

General Description:	*The practice of hoping for a secret desire and believing that it will come true if the wish was made at just the right time.* Examples of such propitious moments include just before blowing out candles on a birthday cake or seeing a shooting star.
Origins:	People have been making wishes too long to allow for a clear origin. As for the related tradition of placing candles on a birthday cake, that custom derives from early Greek culture, in which a round cake was baked

in honor of Artemis, the goddess of the moon. In her honor, a candle lit on top made it glow like the moon.

In Practice: Birthday cake candles are supposed to be blown out with a single breath after making a wish. Wishes come true if the candles are extinguished in one blow, and if the person who makes the wish does not tell anyone else what he or she asked for. The smoke from the extinguished flame then ascends to the heavens, where the wish may be granted. Other fortuitous times to make a wish include when blowing away a fallen eyelash, releasing a ladybug, breaking a wishbone, blowing the fluff from a dandelion head, or throwing a penny into a wishing well.

Cultural
Context: The Make-a-Wish Foundation, a nonprofit organization that grants wishes to children suffering from life-threatening illness, was founded in 1980, the result of seven-year-old Christopher Greicius and his brave battle with leukemia. Chris had always wanted to be a police officer. When his medical condition worsened, a family friend arranged a special day for the young boy. Chris was taken on a helicopter ride and a motorcycle ride and then sworn in as an honorary policeman—truly his wish come true. He died four days later. Realizing how powerful the experience was and how much joy it brought, Chris's mother and two of the participating police officers decided to help more children stricken with life-threatening illnesses.

They started small, granting the wish of another young leukemia patient who wanted to be a firefighter. Over the next few years they raised additional money, granted more wishes, and attracted the attention of the Disney Company. Today, the foundation has granted more than 145,000 wishes and brightened the lives of many children and their families.

| Related Superstitions: | Ladybug, Lucky Penny, Shooting Star, Wishbone |

47. MANEKI NEKO

| Other Name: | Money cat. |

| General Description: | *Japanese for "beckoning cat," this ceramic or porcelain replica of a cat, with one or both front paws raised in a beckoning gesture, is believed to attract money and/or customers for the business owner who displays it.* The statue is usually painted significant colors, and other decorations include a bib or collar, a bell, and a gold coin. |

| Origins: | According to a Japanese folktale, this good-luck charm is based on a real tortoiseshell, a type of cat with distinctive red, black, chocolate, and cinnamon fur patches. The story goes that the cat, who belonged to a temple master during Japan's Edo period (1603–1867), appeared to beckon a wealthy noble- |

man who was one day riding past the cat's rundown temple home. Intrigued, the man dismounted his horse and approached. At that very moment, a lightning bolt struck the ground where he had just stood. Unnerved—and extremely grateful—the man endowed the temple with wealth and lands, and thus a legend was born.

Variations: In many cultures, tricolored or calico cats are considered lucky. Unlike the black cat, these felines are beneficial to own, and if you save one from harm one of your wishes will come true. Sailors thought that male calico cats were harbingers of a safe journey at sea.

In Practice: Maneki Neko are used throughout Japan and China and are often seen in American Chinatowns as well as in homes and offices organized according to the principles of feng shui. The helpful feline figurine is usually placed prominently near an entrance or another location where it can easily attract financial gain: in the window, at the reception desk of a restaurant, or in the back windshield of a taxicab. If the cat's right paw is raised, it is attracting money; if the left paw is raised, it is focusing on bringing customers into an establishment. Money cats are also popular as piggy banks since they will naturally attract coins.

Cultural Context: In 2007 Nike released a unique line of sneakers called the Nike SB Maneki Neko "Money Cat" Dunks.

Available in the traditional colors of the money cat
(white, red, gold, and black), the shoes feature inspi-
rational messages on the tongue, such as "Feeling
Lucky?" and "Get That Money!"

Related
Superstitions:

Black Cat, Nine Lives of Cats

48. **MANTRA**

General
Description:

ॐ

A word, phrase, or sentence used for meditation.
Chanted repeatedly, a mantra helps focus the mind
and channel energies, thus allowing the practitioner
to achieve life goals by tapping into innermost needs
and abilities. It forms an essential part of the Hindu
religion.

Origins:

From the Sanskrit words *man*, meaning "mind" or "to
think," and *tra*, meaning "tool," mantra translates as
"instrument of thought." In ancient India, wise men
called *rishis* were said to have developed mantras from
pure intuition. Today, words, syllables, or phrases
from such sacred writings as the *Bhagavad Gita* are
selected in the hope that their spiritual energies will
manifest themselves in the meditator. Finding your
personal mantra will help bring about your particular
desires and states of consciousness.

Variations: A visual manifestation of the auditory mantra—called a
ॐ †   yantra—is a geometrical design crafted for specific peo-
              ple or gods and goddesses and intended to harness ener-
              gies and bring about realities for those who meditate
              upon them. Christianity has its version of mantras, most
              notably prayers such as "Hail Mary" or "Our Father,"
              which may be repeated a specific number of times to
              obtain absolution, clarity, or assistance in times of crisis.

In Practice: Mantras are most often used by members of the
ॐ ☸   Hindu and Buddhist religions as well as by adherents
              of New Age philosophies. The most famous mantra,
              and the easiest to learn, is the simple word *om* ("I
              am"). Because of its universal application, *om* can be
              recited by anyone at any time for meditation and self-
              realization. To meditate most effectively, set aside a
              room or a corner large enough to place a yoga mat.
              Before beginning, it is appropriate to shower and don
              new, clean, comfortable clothes that will not restrict
              movements or distract the mind. Take several deep
              breaths while sitting in a comfortable position, clear-
              ing your mind of thoughts and worries. Shut yourself
              off from distractions and people and begin meditat-
              ing. Some prefer to close their eyes while reciting a
              mantra to lessen the chance of distraction and to
              encourage spiritual awakening. Others prefer to focus
              on a particular object (such as a yantra), a spot on a
              wall, or a tree in the distance. Simply find your
              mantra and use it to help you achieve your goals.

Cultural
Context:

The notion of mantra meditation became extremely popular in the United States in the 1960s and 1970s. In Woody Allen's classic 1977 film *Annie Hall*, one of the guests at a pretentious Hollywood party calls his meditation guru, saying urgently, "Hello? I forgot my mantra!" This nod to faux spirituality demonstrated the continued weakening of a once-powerful tradition.

In the 1980s, audiotapes featuring calming sounds of rainforest waterfalls and chirping birds were marketed as "subliminal message therapy." Claiming to help people lose weight, make money, gain confidence, or achieve similar positive results, the tapes featured soft-spoken voices whispering such positive statements as "I am a strong, powerful woman" or "I have the ability to stop smoking." Users were instructed to listen to the tapes at bedtime, when human consciousness is at its most relaxed and receptive, as well as while sleeping so that the unconscious mind could easily absorb the affirmations, resulting in a change of habits.

More recently, people have been known to buy "subliminal software"—computer programs that flash messages onscreen so quickly that the conscious mind fails to register them. Subconsciously, however, the flashing communications shower us with confidence, helping to increase productivity and balance spiritual energies.

Related
Superstitions:

Yantra

MASTER NUMBERS

General
Description:

In numerology, the numbers 11, 22, and 33. These digits are stronger manifestations of, and share characteristics with, the single digits 2, 4, and 6. A birth or destiny number of 11 can be further reduced to 2 (since 1 + 1 = 2), just as 22 can be reduced to 4, and 33 to 6.

Origins:

Numerology is an occult science thought to date back to the Greek mathematician Pythagoras (569–470 BCE). Other roots include the ancient Jewish mystic tradition called Kabbalah. Numerologists seek correlations between a person's significant numbers and the planets to which those numbers correspond. Like other numbers in numerology, the master numbers are endowed with particular energies and personality traits.

Variations:

Recently, the classic master numbers (11, 22, 33) have been joined by 44, 55, and 66, although traditional numerologists consider these additions controversial.

In Practice:

People with master numbers inherent in their birth- or destiny-number calculations are considered to be extra intuitive and to possess special traits. Living up to the potential of the master numbers is a more difficult task than it is for single-digit numbers because the former combine the energies of the base number (the sum of the digits) with the higher energies of the double-digit number. The most intuitive number is considered to be 11, which is linked to significant vision. Called the master builder, 22 is a combination of vision and action; 33, the highest number, is known as the master teacher because it seeks to impart guidance to the world.

Cultural Context:

Numerologists had much to say about September 11, 2001, and the terrorist attacks against the United States that occurred on that day. Within weeks of the date, eleven instances of the master number 11 were discovered, leading some to believe that the tragic events were written "in the numbers." The day itself was the eleventh day of the month; the month and day (9 + 1 + 1) equal 11; the first airplane to crash into the towers was American Airlines Flight 11, which contained eleven crew members; the airplane that crashed into the Pentagon was flight number 77 (11 x 7); both the north and south towers of the World Trade Center contained 110 stories; the two buildings standing side-by-side formed an "11"; September 11 is the 254th day of the year (2 + 4 + 5 = 11), after which there are 111 days remaining; and finally, New York was the eleventh state to be added to the union when the thirteen-state confederation separated from England to form the United States.

Related Superstitions:

Astroligical Horoscope, Birth Number, Destiny Number, Vedic Astrology

49. **MEZUZAH**

General
Description:

A text from the Torah (Deuteronomy 6:4–9, 11:13–21) that is handwritten on parchment, rolled, and enclosed within a small case or box. The decorative tubular case may be made of any material, from wood or silver to stone or ceramic, and it is often beautifully carved or painted. The parchment consists of exactly twenty-two lines (corresponding to the number of letters in the Hebrew alphabet) that form the verses from the Shema prayer that begins "Hear, O Israel." The text must be hand copied by a highly trained scribe, who uses a special quill and writes on parchment. Every letter must be complete and unbroken—the slightest crack in the ink invalidates the parchment. On the back, it is common to write *Shaddai*, one of the many names of God, whose letters stand for *Shomer Dlatot Yisrael* ("guarder of the doorposts of Israel"). It is then customary to roll the parchment so that the word shows when the scroll is placed in the case. The whole is then affixed to the right side of doorposts of Jewish homes.

Origins:

The Hebrew word *mezuzah* means "doorpost." The notion of placing a scroll with holy text on the doorposts of one's home and business originates with the biblical commandment in the Old Testament that states: "Inscribe these words upon the doorposts of your house and on your gates" (Deuteronomy 6:9).

The phrase "these words" refers to the major theological statements in the Bible regarding monotheism, the belief in the existence of only one God. According to biblical tradition, if a person believes in the one God and serves him faithfully, he will reward the faithful with rain in season, grass, grain, wine, and oil, all the things needed for a long, healthy life.

In Practice: Mezuzahs are affixed at the front door of most Jewish homes; observant Jews place one at the entry of every room except bathrooms and closets. The mezuzah contains protective qualities, and attaching one properly assures that God will guard the inhabitants' comings and goings. It should be placed on the righthand side of the door, at about eye level and angled slightly inward, toward the room. Because the mezuzah contains holy passages from the Bible that include the name of God, it is traditional to touch the case when passing and then kiss your fingers. This sign of reverence is an acknowledgment of God's presence in your life, which is constant even as you do things as mundane as walking from one room to the next.

Those who adhere strictly to mezuzah traditions bring their scrolls to be examined by an expert every few years, replacing those that are no longer kosher because letters are broken or incomplete due to wear. It is believed that having a nonkosher mezuzah brings with it bad luck and the lack of God's protective regard.

Cultural Context:	In 1967, when Israeli soldiers succeeded in securing the old city of Jerusalem during the Six-Day War, among the first things they did in celebration was to affix large iron mezuzahs on all the gates of the Holy City, a definitive symbol that it was once again under Jewish control.
Related Superstitions:	Comings and Goings

50. **NAZAR BONCUGU (EVIL EYE BEAD)**

General Description:	*A glass amulet that consists of concentric circles of dark blue, light blue, white, and sometimes yellow, thus resembling an eye.* It often takes the form of either a bead or a flat disk. The nazar boncugu is made from sand, iron, copper, water, and salt, all of which are believed to have antievil properties. The materials are melted together in specially built pinewood-burning ovens that reach in excess of 1,600°F (900°C). Used to ward off the evil eye in every context, nazar boncugu are common throughout eastern Mediterranean countries, especially Turkey. They are believed to deflect the negative forces back to their origin, keeping the object of scorn or jealousy free from harm.
Origins:	The concept of the evil eye dates to prebiblical times (see "Evil Eye," page 75). Evil-eye beads are thought

to have originated in ancient Egypt but are first recorded about three thousand years ago in the Anatolia region of Turkey. They continue to be crafted today by revered artisans who have been expertly trained in centuries-old techniques of Mediterranean glassmaking.

Variations: The American equivalent of the evil-eye bead is the pronouncement "I am rubber, you are glue. Whatever you say bounces off me and sticks to you!" In similar fashion, the nazar boncugu is believed to make jealousy and ill will bounce off the victim and stick to those who harbor such negative sentiments.

In Practice: In Mediterranean countries, nazar boncugu are more than mere talismans. Affixed to everything from dashboards to farm animals, they are worn as necklaces, anklets, bracelets, earrings, and rings. They are also incorporated into the foundations of Turkish office buildings and homes and may be included on Web sites or printed on stationery to bring about good luck and prosperity. Responsible Turkish parents do not take their babies anywhere without first adorning them with evil-eye necklaces. Sold in outdoor bazaars and artisanal markets throughout the region (and worldwide via the Internet), the nazar boncugu is a ubiquitous symbol of health and sustenance.

Cultural
Context: Genuine evil-eye beads are always blue, a color believed by many cultures and religious traditions to

bring about good luck. Yet, Turkish people consider a person with blue eyes to be especially dangerous. Those with light eyes are not to be trusted, and using the nazar boncugu around them is essential.

Related
Superstitions: Blue, Evil Eye, Garlic, Hamsa

51. 📷   **NINE LIVES OF CATS**

General
Description: *The widely held belief that cats die and return to life*
               nine times before expiring for good.

Origins: Several theories exist to explain why cats are presumed to have nine lives. The most obvious is that felines have the uncanny ability to survive falls from great heights and to escape other traumatic events that would certainly kill or seriously injure other animals or humans. They seem to be immortal. Cats are also associated with the ancient Egyptian goddess Bast, daughter of the sun god Ra; in ancient Egyptian art, Bast is typically depicted as a woman with a cat's head, and she is loosely associated with the number 9. As the product of three times three, nine was closely linked to the concept of multiple lives because it is the trinity of trinities, the ultimate manifestation of rebirth. Finally, occult legends purport that witches can turn into cats as many as nine times before exhausting the trick.

Variations: In Arabic and Turkish proverbs, cats are said to have merely seven lives.

In Practice: Kittens are known for their fearless acrobatics. The owner of a new cat may panic when Snowball, who's not much bigger than the palm of a human hand, manages to claw her way up the side of a chair and onto the tabletop, a sign of her reckless pursuit of investigating. Although you may worry that curiosity will indeed kill the cat, take comfort in the knowledge that your inquisitive pet can survive at least nine major tumbles and accidents.

Biological reasons also explain why cats are so nimble and hardy. Physiologically, felines are prepared to survive falls from great heights because of their small size and low body weight, which distributes the impact of a fall throughout their compact and muscular bodies. Furthermore, cats are graced with an innate, highly advanced sense of balance, which enables them to right themselves midair and ensures that they (almost) always land on their feet.

Cultural Context: In George Herriman's comic strip "Krazy Kat" (1913–1940s), the lead character is constantly hit in the head by bricks launched by Ignatz Mouse, with whom Krazy Kat is in love. Offissa Pupp, who, in turn, loves Krazy Kat, tries to catch the bricks as often as possible. Even so, the projectiles that hit their mark likely sent poor Krazy Kat through several of his nine lives during the three decades of the cartoon's existence.

Another famous cartoon cat is Tom, of Tom and Jerry fame, the MGM/Hanna Barbera animated cat and mouse. In one of their earliest adventures, "Fraidy Cat" (1942), Tom uses up nearly all his precious nine lives when Jerry rigs a white cloth in a vacuum cleaner and convinces Tom that it's a ghost. After having heard a scary ghost story on the radio, Tom is especially susceptible to the mouse's wily antics.

Related Superstitions:

Black Cat, Maneki Neko

52. **OPENING AN UMBRELLA INSIDE**

General Description:

Unfurling and opening a specially designed canopied device, which protects the user from rain, while inside a building, vehicle, or other enclosure. This act is believed to bring bad luck not only to the person who performed it but also to the location.

Origins:

Back when umbrellas—also called parasols—were used not to shelter people from rain but to shield them from harsh sunlight, it was thought that opening one indoors would insult the sun gods. After all, structures with roofs are shaded, so carrying an open umbrella inside would imply that the sun's rays were not especially powerful (that is, that umbrellas were just for show, indoors or out). Angered, the sun gods would wreak havoc on the places where they had been insulted, not to mention on the brazen individual who dared offend them.

Variations: It is also bad luck to present an umbrella as a gift, to drop one on the floor, and to lay one on a tabletop or bed.

In Practice: Even if a storm is raging outside, do not open your umbrella until you cross the threshold. Your first steps may be wet ones, but the risk pales in comparison with the inauspicious alternative.

Cultural Context: On the 2006 reality show *American Inventor*, Sheryl McDonald was one of twelve finalists. Her invention was the "Inbrella," a device that inverted and collapsed into a hollow tube inside the handle. Inspired by many a wet pant leg due to closing a traditional umbrella while climbing into her car on rainy days, McDonald created an instrument that allowed the consumer to stay dry while also providing an alternative to throwing a sopping-wet umbrella on the vehicle floor. The question is: Can you open an inverted umbrella inside without incurring bad luck?

53. 📷 **OUIJA BOARD**

General
Description:

A rectangular board printed with the letters of the alpha-bet, the numbers 0–9, and the words "Yes," "No," and "Good Night." Also known as a spirit board or talking board, the Ouija board is used to channel the spirits of the dead and allow them to spell out messages for the living.

Origins:

The Ouija board game was invented in the United States in 1886 after forty years of experimentation with prototypes. Patented in 1891, the board went through several manifestations before being sold in 1966 to Parker Brothers, which continues to manufacture and sell it in varied venues, from toy stores to occult shops. Several inventors and owners of toy companies have claimed to know the origin of the word *ouija*. One argued that a spirit came to him via the board and told him that it was the ancient Egyptian word for "good luck." Although untrue, that explanation is still given. Another theory is that the name is a composite of the French and German words for "yes": *oui* and *ja*.

In Practice:

It is best to practice on a Ouija board in a calm and quiet space, without distraction. Two or more people sit with the board placed on a table between them or with it resting firmly on the edges of their knees. Using a wooden message indicator called a planchette, the players become conduits for a conjured spirit, which directs them to point to various letters, one after the other, spelling out answers to questions. Each person lightly places an index and middle finger on the planchette, and one person asks, "Is anyone there?" Once the presence of a spirit is confirmed, either through the message "yes" or an unmistakable feeling of otherworldly presence, other questions are asked. This sequence works best if players have entered a séancelike trance, open to acting as conduits to the spirits guidings their hands. Practitioners of the Ouija board confess that after several tries, they begin to feel a spirit move them—literally. Their hand will begin to move the planchette, although they may feel like they're not in control of their movements. They then sense when the spirit wants to stop, allowing their hands to rest at a particular location. One of the players jots down the letters or numbers at which the spirit stops, and later everyone tries to decipher the messages. This task is sometimes difficult, for spirits don't always spell words completely; they make liberal use of abbreviation and phonetic spelling and sometimes communicate in code. Once the message is delivered, it is up to you to decide whether to accept the information and act on it accordingly.

Cultural Context:

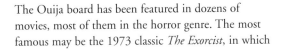

The Ouija board has been featured in dozens of movies, most of them in the horror genre. The most famous may be the 1973 classic *The Exorcist*, in which the ghost of Captain Howdy uses one to take over the body of Regan. A Ouija board is also featured in *Tales from the Crypt* (1972) and the *Witchboard* trilogy (1985, 1992, 1995). In addition to these scary representations, the board was used to bring good into the world in the heartwarming 1990 film *Awakenings*, starring Robin Williams and Robert De Niro, which was based on a true story about Dr. Oliver Sacks. De Niro plays the catatonic Leonard Lowe, one of the victims of an encephalitis epidemic that left him severely brain damaged and unable to speak, walk, or communicate in any way since childhood. When given a Ouija board, however, Leonard uses it to spell out a message, leading Dr. Malcolm Sayer to recognize that his mind is alive. The doctor then fights for permission to give Leonard an experimental drug called L-Dopa, which brings him back into consciousness.

Related Superstitions:

Fortune-Teller

54. **PALM READING**

General Description:

The art of interpreting the lines on the palm as well as the shape of the hands, fingers, and nails to determine a person's traits and talents. A palm reading can also reveal details about one's fate and future. Palm readers consider how the unique aspects of one's hands relate to a person's tendencies, abilities, relationships, genetic composition, and character.

Origins: According to Lori Reid, author of *The Art of Hand Reading*, the history of palm reading dates to at least 3000 BCE, although conceivably it was a part of Stone Age culture as well. About that date, the emperor of China used his thumbprint to seal documents, a nod to the use of hand imagery in ancient Chinese, Egyptian, and Indian cultures. References to the interpretations of hands are first found in Sanskrit texts dating from about 2000 BCE. Palmistry is also alluded to in Vedic scripts, the Bible, and early Semitic writings. In the 300s BCE in Egypt, Aristotle discovered a manuscript on the subject and ordered it sent to Alexander the Great, who recognized the material's importance and had it translated into Latin. From that text, palm reading made its way into Western culture and, by the first millennium, was firmly established there. Throughout history, the art of palmistry has faced many detractors. Despite being banned, it has continued to bounce back, experiencing revivals in popularity. Today, it is accepted as a valid New Age spiritual practice.

Variations: Palmistry is divided into several subcategories, in which different readers can specialize. Chirognomy is the study of the shape of hands; chiromancy is the study of the lines and markings on hands; and dermatoglyphics is the study of skin patterns.

In Practice: A true palm reader will pay attention to the "whole package"—noting everything about your hands, not just the overly hyped "life line." The reader will look at the overall shape, determining if you have pointed, square, conical, spadelike, or mixed hands. The shapes correspond to the basic elements of earth, air, fire, and water, which in turn indicate basic character traits. The reader will also analyze the length and width of your fingers, the spaces between them, the growth patterns and shapes of your fingernails, the texture of your skin, and the pads at the base of your palm. Finally, he or she will look at the many lines you possess—your life, head, heart, health, fate, fame, marriage, money, sex, spirit, travel, and luck lines, among others—to read into your life so far and inform you what may be in store for your future.

The reader will also distinguish between your right and left hands since each reveals different aspects of your personality and spirit. The dominant hand (which, for most, is the right hand) represents a person's mature adult self, the conscious being, the public persona that reveals particular talents and potential. The nondominant or passive hand reveals the subconscious self, the private and intimate side, childhood tendencies, and genetic dispositions. The thumb is considered the most significant finger of all, pointing to a person's basic sense of determination and will.

The lines, as shown in illustration 54, are:

- Line 1: The **life line** begins between your thumb and index finger and curves to the base of the thumb, near the wrist. It indicates the number of years you will live, the strength of your health and vitality, and the basic nature of your personality.

- Line 2: The **head line** sits just above the life line and cuts across the middle of your palm. It represents your intellectual leanings and your personal philosophies. Depending on the line's shape and other properties, it can also reveal details about your attention span and other mental tendencies.

- Line 3: The **heart line** is above the head line, beginning around the base of the index or middle finger and extending across the palm to the pinky. It represents your emotional nature and the various properties of your love life, past, present, and future.

- Line 4: The **fate line** runs vertically up the middle of the palm. It indicates your basic destiny in this lifetime. Its character can reveal how much of an influence the outside world has on you, that is, if you are self-reliant and in control of your fate.

- Line 5: The **fame line** is parallel to, and sometimes joined with, the fate line. Many palms lack this line, which may explain why so few of us achieve public acknowledgment of our accomplishments and talents.

- Line 6: The **marriage line** (or lines) is the short horizontal line just below the base of the pinky. If you have more than one, chances are you will marry more than once. The nearer the pinky the line sits, the later in life marriage will occur. Various forks and breaks in the lines can represent marital problems or divorce, and branching lines symbolize children.

Cultural
Context:

Don't have time to sit through a lengthy palm reading? No problem. Online readers offer a service by which you use a computer scanner to photograph your hand, save it as a jpeg file, and e-mail it along with a fee paid via a major credit card. Within a week, you will receive an email containing your personalized analysis.

Related
Superstitions:

Fortune-Teller, Psychic

PSYCHICS

Other Name:

Mediums.

General
Description:

From the Greek word psychikos, *meaning "of the soul/mind"* (psyche *means "soul" in Greek*). A person imbued with the ability to connect with other realms of consciousness. Through telepathy (nonverbal communication), extrasensory perception (ESP), clairvoyance (in which the future can be foretold), and other innate talents, psychics can read into the future as well as the past to help determine how someone should act in the present. Psychics are able to channel the spirits of the deceased and to predict future events.

Origins:
Like fortune-tellers, psychics have likely existed in some form for centuries. Although some psychics hone their skills over years of practicing their art, it is widely accepted that people are either born with this gift or not.

In Practice:
Have you ever had a feeling that the phone was about to ring before it actually does? Have you ever sensed who was on the other line? Experiences like these are merely an inkling of what a true psychic feels every day. Beyond foretelling mundane facts, psychics claim to predict significant future events, such as what team will win the Super Bowl or how international conflicts will be resolved. Seek advice from a psychic if you are at an impasse regarding a major decision or if you need simple clarification about the direction your life is taking.

Cultural Context:

In the television drama series *Medium*, actress Patricia Arquette portrays Allison DuBois, a real-life research medium who works for a district attorney's office. DuBois was born with the ability to see and speak to dead people and foresee the future; her dreams contain information about violent crimes, which she then tries to prevent or solve. Police departments do sometimes employ psychics to help them solve particularly difficult mysteries, and DuBois has authored several books about her experiences.

Related
Superstitions:

Fortune-Teller, Palm Reading

55. **RABBIT'S FOOT**

General
Description:
☺

The dried and preserved appendage of a rabbit. The soft and furry amulet is commonly attached to key chains or carried in the back left pocket to bring good luck to the owner.

Origins:
✿
ꙮ

Rabbits have been described as lucky animals in many cultures, mainly because of their ability to reproduce prolifically. Long associated with fertility and spring, the season of rebirth and fecundity, the rabbit has been used as a symbol for good luck in childbearing. But along with its sunny, happy image, the rabbit also has a darker manifestation among the superstitious. Because rabbits spend a good part of the year huddled in underground burrows, they have been associated with evil spirits and witches; therefore the good luck linked to them is more directly linked to killing them. It is from this line of thinking that the prevalent symbol of the rabbit's foot originates. Beginning in the 1600s, West African slaves forced to travel to American colonies brought with them their beliefs in a system of magic called hoodoo, in which the rabbit's foot serves as a prominent talisman against evil forces.

In Practice: Today, rabbits' feet are often dyed bright colors and attached to key chains. They are used worldwide but are especially popular in places where gambling is practiced, such as Las Vegas, Nevada. There, you will likely see hopeful gamblers rubbing their lucky rabbits' feet before casting dice or placing bets. It should also be noted that most of the contemporary examples are faux, for animal rights movements have made great strides to ban the killing of innocent animals for the purpose of bringing luck to humans. According to hoodoo beliefs, however, only a real rabbit foot—and, notably, the left hind foot—will do the trick. Other sources purport that a rabbit's foot becomes increasingly lucky if it was obtained from a rabbit shot in a cemetery with a silver bullet under a full moon on a Friday by a cross-eyed shooter—or any combination thereof.

Cultural   In the 2006 movie *Mission Impossible III*, Tom Cruise
Context: plays Ethan Hunt, a reluctant IMF (Impossible Mission Force) agent who is called back into active duty when his protégé is killed in the field. To solve the case that his colleague was tracking when he died,

Ethan must find and decode a hazardous biomaterial called the "Rabbit's Foot." His quest for the mysterious object and its maniacal owners takes him to Berlin and Shanghai, where both he and his unsuspecting fiancée are nearly killed—though, of course, they manage to escape alive and well. Perhaps that rabbit's foot brought good luck after all.

Related
Superstitions:

Voodoo Dolls

56. 📷 **RED STRING**

General
Description:
🤛

A red-colored string worn as a bracelet on the left wrist that, according to new Kabbalists, fends off the evil eye and protects the wearer from harm.

Origins:
✡ ✻

Although today the widespread popularity of the red string bracelet is linked with Kabbalah, in the ancient Jewish body of mysticism, traditions involving red strings are related to another text: the Bible. It was originally thought that by wrapping a long red string around the tomb of the matriarch Rachel in Bethlehem, and then cutting that string into many smaller sections, the resulting bracelets would be endowed with a protective energy. Because Rachel is associated specifically with images of fertility, these strings were used by

Israeli women to help them survive pregnancy and childbirth.

Variations: In Chinese culture, red is the ultimate color of luck. Chinese brides wear red dresses on their wedding day; the dragon of the Chinese New Year celebration is made of red materials; and within the system of feng shui, red strings are used to hang crystals and to release bad luck from a house (by hanging four red strings from the floor to the ceiling in each corner of the bedroom).

In Practice: For a mere $26, you too can own a mystical red string, now available online. The Kabbalah Centre, with physical locations worldwide as well as a Web site, sells the string together with an explanatory book on the subject. Some jewelry stores also now carry sterling silver bracelets with red strings woven into them. Another option is to travel to Jerusalem and visit the Western Wall. There, beggars carrying dozens of strings, some of which are decorated with evil-eye beads or hamsas, will tie one around your wrist and offer you blessings—all for mere pennies. Once you've attained your red string, be sure that someone you love ties it onto your left wrist (the left side of the body is the receiving side, according to Kabbalah), followed by six successive knots, for a total of seven. Recite a prayer of protection and promise yourself that you will refuse to succumb to negative thoughts, and then go on your way, secure in the knowledge that you are protected. Note that you should never remove the string. It should fall off on its own after months of wear and tear, a sign that it's time to begin anew.

Cultural Context:

Kabbalah has recently been all the rage in Hollywood, surpassing even Scientology in its ability to attract a coterie of famous followers. Britney Spears, Demi Moore, Roseanne Barr, and David Beckham have all been spotted wearing red strings. However, perhaps the most noticeable red-string-sporting celebrity is Madonna, who for years has been a devotee of the Kabbalah Center. Not only does Madonna (or Esther, as she sometimes prefers to be called) wear her red string religiously, she also makes sure that enough Kabbalah water (blessed and meditated upon so that the liquid is spiritually pure and balanced) is available for herself and her staff while on tour.

Related Superstitions:

Feng Shui, Hamsa, Nazar Boncugu

57. **RIGHT FOOT FIRST**

General Description:

The act of placing the terminal appendage of the right leg before that of the left leg to ensure getting off to a good start.

Origins: In the Middle Ages, knights mounted their horses
                with the right foot because they believed that the left
                side of the body was inherently negative and unlucky.
                This tradition was passed through the generations
                until it became second nature. It should also be noted
                that in Islamic rituals, right always comes before
                left—specifically for ablutions in the morning and
                before prayer, when the right hand and foot are
                washed before the left.

Variations: The tradition of carrying a bride over a threshold on
                her wedding day may also stem from this preference
                for right-footedness. It was considered a bad omen for
                a bride to enter her new home on the left foot, and so
                she was encouraged to step over the threshold with
                her right foot first. In her nervousness, she might trip
                while trying to alter her gait. Tripping, however,
                would be even unluckier than stepping with the left
                foot first, hence the tradition of sweeping her off her
                feet and carrying her over the threshold.

In Practice: The related expressions "getting off on the right foot,"
                "waking up on the wrong side of the bed," and "put-
                ting your best foot forward" all stem from the super-
                stition that it is good luck to begin most processes
                with your right foot and bad to do so with the left.
                You should always enter a home or board a boat with
                your right foot first, and mounting a horse should
                never be done with the left.

Should you get up on the wrong side of the bed—stepping out of bed on your left foot—to avoid bad luck for the day, you must put on the sock and shoe of your right foot before your left one. To reverse the bad luck that's sure to follow if you step onto a boat with your left foot, retrace your steps backward; remove your shoes, placing your right shoe on the left foot and vice versa; and try again, this time with your right foot first.

Cultural
Context:

David Beckham, the legendary British soccer player who inspired the movie *Bend It Like Beckham* and is the hero of sports fans (and Posh Spice fans) world-wide, is known for his powerful right foot. His talent for kicking a ball straight into the goal zone, with just the right curve to circumvent the goalkeeper, is entirely dependent on his right foot.

Related
Superstitions:

Carrying a Bride over a Threshold

---

58.   **ROSARY**

General
Description:
†

A string of beads organized into groups of ten that is used for prayer rituals in the Catholic faith; it is generally dedicated to the Virgin Mary. The term *rosary* applies to both the beads as well as the sets of prayers and meditations. A rosary usually consists of five decades, or groups of ten beads, separated by a single, larger bead. This grouping corresponds to the ten Hail Mary prayers and one Lord's Prayer recited during meditation. Between these is recited the Catholic doxology that begins "Glory Be to the Father." Also on the rosary are a cross, which corresponds to the act of making the sign of the cross, and five additional beads for prayers. The rosary may be made from a variety of natural or synthetic materials, including wood, stone, metal, plastic, and bone. Many sets are blessed and thus treated with great respect.

Origins: From the Latin word *rosarium*, meaning "crown of roses," the rosary likely arose during the earliest days of Christianity, when prayer ropes were common. It replaced an earlier tradition of a daily recitation of the 150 psalms of the Bible, which were broken into groups of ten and fifty. Its current form and prayer order were established by the late sixteenth century.

Variations: In Mexico, brides and grooms are encircled and sometimes tied together by long strings of rosary beads, a symbol of their new unity. In Greece, sets of beads called *komboloi* (also known as "worry beads") are rubbed anytime day or night to ensure safe travel, good health, and diversion of the evil eye. The Greek beads are thought to be a secular variation of the prayer beads carried by Greek Orthodox monks.

In Practice: Devout Catholics aim to say between 150 and 200 prayers every day, using rosary beads to help them keep track of and count the prayers. Some of the faithful carry the beads at all times. Others are less fastidious about their prayers but feel that carrying rosary beads will bring good luck and protect them from evil forces. To aid the reciter in accomplishing the requisite number of daily prayers, the rosary is divided into decades. Furthermore, within the rosary there are twenty mysteries, or topics of meditation, which are divided into four groups of five. These groupings are known as the Joyful Mysteries (recited on Mondays and Saturdays), Luminous Mysteries (recited on Thursdays), Sorrowful Mysteries (recited on Tuesdays and Fridays), and Glorious Mysteries (recited on Wednesdays and Sundays). Each mystery prompts followers to meditate on specific miraculous events and biblical passages that relate to faith and daily life.

Many Catholics choose to recite the rosary while in a church, but the meditation may be performed in any situation if one has the proper frame of mind. The most complete recitation follows the steps below.

1. Holding the cross at the end of the rosary, make the sign of the cross and say the "Apostles Creed."

2. At the first bead, say the "Our Father" prayer.

3. Say a "Hail Mary" prayer at each of the next three beads.

4. In the section before the next bead, say the "Glory Be to the Father" prayer.

5. Announce the mystery and then say the "Our Father."

6. At each of the next ten beads, say the "Hail Mary" while meditating on the mystery.

7. In the section before the larger bead, say the "Glory Be to the Father" prayer and announce the mystery for the next decade.

8. At the larger bead, say the "Our Father." Repeat steps 6–8.

Cultural Context: For those who want to remember to recite daily prayers but don't want to tote around a jangling string of beads in a pocket, a solution exists. Get a rosary tattoo. Nicole Richie has one on her foot, and Alyssa Milano "carries" her beads on the back of her right shoulder.

Related Superstitions: Cross, Evil Eye

59. 📷 **RUNES**

General
Description:
⚪

An ancient alphabet script called Futhark that is used as a method of divination. Each letter of Futhark, called a rune, is also a word imbued with a distinct meaning in a Germanic language and a specific mystical meaning. Carved into a stone or ceramic tile, runes are drawn by a spiritual seeker to find answers to existential questions or keys to the future. Like tarot cards or the *I Ching*, runes are used as fortune-telling aids.

Origins:

From the Gothic word *runa*, meaning "mystery," runes were first used in the first century in Northern Europe and Scandinavia, notably Germany, Ireland, Norway, and Iceland. The practice continued until the Middle Ages, when it fell out of fashion during the Christianization of Europe and the spread of Latin. They were officially banned by the Roman Catholic Church in 1639.

Historians assume that the Futhark alphabet was intended for mystical use more than as a language. In fact, there is no evidence that Futhark was ever used as a spoken language; instead, it was carved into stones to convey messages and fortunes. Norse mythology posits that runes were invented by the god Odin, who envisioned them while hanging for nine days on his own sword. Vikings and Celts are said to have used runes to help guide their travels.

Runic letters survived the Church's banishment in

Sweden, where they were used throughout the centuries. In most European countries, however, the letters remained unused until their revival in the 1920s and 1930s by the Nazi party in Germany, which used runic symbols for their S.S. logos. Due to the negative connotations resulting from affiliation with that organization, runes again fell out of fashion. It was not until the New Age movements of the 1980s that runes were reclaimed as a tool for spiritual awakening and self-improvement.

In Practice: Each character of the twenty-four-letter Futhark alphabet is inscribed on a tile, which carries specific divination meanings (see table on page 184).

As in Scrabble, the runes are first placed in a dark bag. While contemplating a question or issue that you would like to resolve or gain insight into, place your hand in the bag. Without looking, draw a number of tiles and place them in a specific order before you, keeping them in exactly the orientation that they were drawn. That is, if you draw a tile with the letter facing down and the blank side up, place it exactly that way. If the next one emerges upside down and backward, do not straighten it. The way in which each tile is drawn has specific implications for your reading.

Depending on your level of expertise (and patience), you may draw one, three, or five runes. In a single draw, the rune will represent every aspect of the issue at hand. In a three-rune draw, arrange the tiles

Rune	Futhark Letter	Meaning
ᚠ	Fehu	Money, finances, possessions; material goods or wealth
ᚢ	Uruz	Strength, virility
ᚦ	Thurisaz	Gateway, beginning
ᚨ	Ansuz	A message or signal, a secret; speech
ᚱ	Raido	Travel, sojourn, movement
ᚲ	Kaunaz	Openings, shedding of light on something, fire
ᚷ	Gibo	A gift of blessing; partnerships
ᚹ	Wunjo	Joy, happiness, illumination
ᚺ	Jagalaz	Disruption, chaos, shattering of illusion
ᚾ	Nauthiz	Pain, confinement, limitation
ᛁ	Isa	Inaction
ᛃ	Jera	Fertility, harvesting, returns; reaping what you've sown
ᛇ	Eihwaz	Protection, defense; also withdrawal or barriers
ᛈ	Perth	Secrets, initiations, occult or hidden things
ᛉ	Algiz	Defense, protection
ᛊ	Sowelu	Completion, perfection
ᛏ	Twiwaz (Tyr)	Victory, conquest
ᛒ	Berkana	Renewal, rebirth, new beginnings
ᛖ	Ehwaz	Overcoming barriers, movement, progressions
ᛗ	Mannaz	The self, humanity
ᛚ	Leguz	Water, sea, motherhood; intuition
◇	Inguz	Fertility, birth, beginnings
ᛞ	Dagaz	Sunlight, enlightenment
ᛟ	Othela	The home, hearth, possessions

in a horizontal row, placing the first rune on your right side, representing the present; the second in the center, symbolizing action; and the third on your left, to represent outcome. These three runes will provide a more complete picture of what you are going to do and how it will impact your life. For a five-rune draw, place them, one at a time, in a vertical row, successively from top to bottom. The five runes stand for the overview, challenge, action to be taken, sacrifice to be made, and outcome of the situation. Once the runes are drawn and carefully placed in the correct order, consult one of the many guides or books that interpret runes in all their potential positions. With time, you will gain an intuitive sense of what a specific rune means for you.

Cultural Context:
In 1898 a farmer named Olaf Ohman found a large stone slab buried on his property in Alexandria, Minnesota. Known as the Kensington Runestone, the rock bore cryptic engravings that historians have since deciphered as being a Viking language dated to 1362. The text describes a journey that expands our historical knowledge of Norse exploration in North America at that time. Although some have claimed that the runestone is a hoax, it is still considered a valid historical artifact and is on display at the Runestone Museum in Alexandria.

Related Superstitions:
Fortune-Teller, I Ching, Tarot Cards

60. **SCARAB**

General
Description:

A type of beetle of the family Scarabaeidae. Also known as the dung beetle, the scarab is most famous for rolling balls of its own excrement, using its antennae and front legs, and placing the ball in burrows where it lays eggs. Once the larvae appear, they eat the dung until they grow enough to emerge from the holes. The scarab is a good-luck charm and can be worn as an amulet to protect against evil forces.

Origins:

In ancient Egypt, the scarab was worshipped as a god called Khepril, meaning "one who has come into being." Because Egyptians presumed that scarabs spontaneously self-created from dung, the insects were associated with Atum, the god of creation. The scarab's raylike antenna and the act of rolling balls of dung across the ground reminded the Egyptians of the sun god, and so the insect is often depicted pushing a sun across the sky.

In Practice:

Scarab amulets were worn by ancient Egyptians as good-luck charms on necklaces, engraved in stone seals, and placed on the chest of a corpse as part of the mummification process. In this last practice, the insect took the form of carved "heart scarabs," which were believed to aid the soul of the deceased on its journey to the afterlife.

Cultural
Context:

The largest dung beetle measures five feet (91.5 cm) long and three feet (152.5 cm) tall and is made entirely of stone. It is a statue that dates from the Ptolemaic period (305 BCE–30 BCE), and it once stood in an ancient Egyptian temple. The artifact later traveled to Istanbul (which was then Constantinople, the capital of the Roman Empire) and eventually made its way to London, where it now resides in the halls of the British Museum.

Related
Superstitions:

Charm Bracelet

61. 📷 **SHOOTING STAR**

General
Description:

Meteorites (dust and rock matter) that burn as they fall through earth's atmosphere, thus resembling stars "shoot-ing" across the sky.

Origins:

The tradition of wishing upon a shooting star may stem from a nineteenth-century American nursery rhyme: "Star light, star bright, First star I see tonight / I wish I may, I wish I might / Have the wish I wish tonight."

In Practice:
☺

If you make a wish while watching a shooting star streak through the night sky, your wish will come true. Even if you can't manage to utter a wish in the few seconds before the light disappears, rest assured that it is good luck just to have seen one. Catching that fleeting glimpse means that you were in the right place at the right time, looking up at just the right spot. That, in itself, bodes well.

To increase your chances of seeing a shooting star, venture outdoors on a clear night, as close as possible to dawn. Try to find a location far from cities, for ambient light will hinder your view. The best locations for a stargazing mission are rural and mountainous landscapes, where you can usually see a lot of stars; even better is to choose a date when meteor showers are at their most frequent. Recline on the ground and search for a patch of sky that strikes your fancy. Then wait for a trail of blazing fire to mark its trajectory across the heavens. Be sure to make a wish!

Cultural Context:

♫

The phrase "shooting star" has come to mean not only "particles of dust falling from outer space through the atmosphere" but "a go-getter, a person who is sure to be successful" as well as a "fleeting experience of intense emotion." These connotations, coupled with its catchy sound, have made for some memorable lines of poetry, and even better song lyrics. Artists as diverse as Ashanti, Bad Company, Bob Dylan, and Elton John have recorded hits titled "Shooting Star." The Disney theme song, "When You Wish Upon a Star," also comes from the traditional reaction to a shooting star. In the botanical world, the spectacularly flowered herbaceous plants of the genus *Dodecatheon* enjoy the common name shooting star.

Related
Superstitions:

Making a Wish

SOMETHING OLD, SOMETHING NEW, SOMETHING BORROWED, SOMETHING BLUE

General
Description:
☺

A common tradition among Western brides to wear an item in each of the four categories: old, new, borrowed, blue. Doing so ensures good luck not only on their wedding day but throughout their marriage as well.

Origins:

This oft-spoken rhyme originated in Victorian England, where the full expression was "Something old, something new, something borrowed, something blue, and a silver sixpence in her shoe." Unfortunately, the sixpence coin is no longer minted in Britain, hence the reference has been eliminated from the saying. Something old represents continuity with one's family; something new hints at hope for the future; something borrowed helps transfer the luck from someone else's happy marriage to yours; something blue symbolizes fidelity and love; and the original sixpence symbolized financial security. Since money is one of the major divisive issues in marriage these days, a return to that tradition may be in order.

Variations: In Ireland, some brides choose their gowns as the "something blue." Much like white is today, blue was associated with purity in ancient times, particularly the purity of the Virgin Mary. In ancient Israel, brides wove blue ribbons into their wedding gowns as a sign of their fidelity, love, and modesty.

In Practice: The most common "something old" is a wedding gown—specifically, one passed down from mother to daughter. If you don't fancy Mom's old-fashioned gown and opt for your dress to be the "something new," then choose a hankerchief or family heirloom as the "old" item. Usually a piece of jewelry is borrowed; it should belong to a close friend or family member of either the bride or groom, preferably someone who is happily married. The blue item is generally relegated to more private bridal attire—namely, the garter. Today's groom may feel compelled to lift his bride's gown as far as decency will allow, in front of hundreds of guests, to retrieve the blue garter and toss it into a crowd of eager single men (the male version of the bride's bouquet toss), but the original notion was more private and personal. To substitute for the silver sixpence, insert a lucky coin (one that retains the silver color) in the heel of the bride's left shoe to ensure wealth in the new marriage.

Cultural Context:

In a classic *Friends* episode, Monica and Chandler make a bet in Las Vegas that if she rolls another eight in her lucky streak at the craps table, they will wed that very night. When she does indeed get two fours on her next roll of the dice, the couple runs to the Vegas chapel. But Monica decides she can't get married until they find the four necessary somethings, so they hasten to the gift shop. Chandler spots a blue sweater, and declares it's both new and blue. For something old, he points out that he has a condom he's been carrying in his wallet since he was twelve years old. Finally, they decide to "borrow" the new blue sweater from the gift shop, stuffing it under Monica's shirt. However, upon arriving at the casino's white chapel, the eager pair has to wait for the previous couple to finish their wedding. The doors open and who should emerge but fellow friends Ross and Rachel—drunk and married! The rest is television history.

Related Superstitions:

Blue, Carrying a Bride over a Threshold, Grooms Seeing Brides

62.

SPILLING SALT

General Description:

To accidentally overturn a salt shaker or otherwise drop or scatter the seasoning. This common sign of bad luck may portend a death in the family.

Origins: In the days when salt was a precious and rare com-
modity (in some parts of the world, one more expensive than gold), carelessly spilling it was thought to
indicate that the devil was coming after your wealth.
To ward off evil forces, it was necessary to throw a
pinch of salt into the devil's eyes. The best method
was to toss the seasoning over the left shoulder, where
he was presumed to be lurking, waiting for the opportunity to afflict the unsuspecting victim. Salt was also
used for medicinal purposes during the Middle Ages,
another reason it was treated with care (and perhaps
why the devil was on the prowl).

Variations: In ancient Rome, soldiers received their wages in salt
rather than monetary currency. This custom led to the
expression "He's not worth his salt," as in, "His work
is not worth what we pay him." Another superstition
involves placing salt crystals in a pouch, worn either
around the neck or in a pocket, as a means of warding
off the evil eye.

In Practice: Toss a pinch of the spilled salt over your left shoulder
to foil the devil's plans and reverse any bad luck that
may have been headed toward you. In addition, some
people contend that to keep the bad luck at bay, you
need to cry enough tears to dissolve the spilled salt.

Cultural   Between 1495 and 1498, Leonardo da Vinci painted
Context: his famous fresco titled *The Last Supper* on a wall in

the convent of Santa Maria delle Grazie in Milan, Italy. It depicts the final gathering of Jesus and his apostles as well as the moment at which Judas's betrayal is revealed. In the scene, Judas has knocked over a salt cellar, spilling the contents onto the table. If ever there was an indicator of bad luck to come, that was it!

SPITTING

General Description:

The act of expelling extra saliva via the mouth. Expectorating in this manner is a way to ward off the evil eye, death, and disease. It has also been used to make an offering to the gods and to aid in promise making and battle waging.

Origins:

In an 1890 article in the *Journal of American Folklore*, Fanny Bergen traces the North American custom of spitting three times on an animal carcass (presumably to avoid catching the same disease that killed the animal). She dates the practice to the time of Pliny, in ancient Rome, when spitting was though to be sufficient action to avoid disease. Spit was thought to be a manifestation of the soul, and, therefore, spitting became a way of presenting an offering to gods—a gift from one's innermost essence. In exchange, the Romans hoped to receive good health. During the same historical period, soldiers customarily spit on their hands before battle, hoping that this infusion from the soul would produce a stronger fist that would remain steady during battle. This practice may be the original version of boxers spitting on their gloves before a match or baseball pitchers' tendency to spit before launching a throw.

In Practice:
There are many different ways to employ spit for the purposes of luck. Greek women are known to spit three times after discussing their children or grandchildren, or anything else precious to them, to stave off the jealous evil eye. Jewish women tend to skip the spitting, choosing instead to utter "pooh, pooh, pooh," which serves the same purpose. In Ireland, the father of a newborn baby is instructed to spit on the infant to scare away the Devil. The Swedish avert the bad luck associated with a black cat crossing their path by spitting three times over the left shoulder. Finally, if you want to seal a deal but are reluctant to prick your finger and mingle blood with your partner's (another common superstitious practice), opt for spitting into your hand before shaking on it.

Cultural Context:
One of the most endearing characters of the 1990s was Mike Myers's Linda Richman, a regular character on *Saturday Night Live*. Based on Myers's real-life Jewish mother-in-law from New York, Linda hosted a show called "Coffee Talk." In one of the first sketches,

she is filling in for the regular host, Paul Baldwin. She starts out with the toned-down version of spitting to avoid the evil eye: "Pawl Baldwin is still sick—pooh, pooh, pooh. He's got schpilkis of the genectagezoink."

Related
Superstitions:

Black Cat, Evil Eye

SYNCHRONICITY

General
Description:
☺

The experience of multiple, simultaneous occurrences that seem to be meaningfully linked to one another, with no logical explanation. A "coincidence" that feels much deeper than mere chance, true synchronicity is a sign of deep psychological awareness and good luck.

Origins:

In 1952 Swiss psychiatrist Carl Jung (1875–1961) published "Synchronicity: An Acausal Connecting Principle," an academic paper on the subject (a term he coined). After spending many years studying the phenomenon, Jung argued that there was a "collective unconscious," a body of knowledge that extended beyond the finite mind, included the forces of the universe, and spanned diverse cultures. According to Jung, what may seem like pure chance is in fact a coincidence manifested by parallel events occurring simultaneously for a definite reason.

In Practice: You reach for a book on the top of your bookcase, and, along with the book (and copious amounts of dust), a photograph of you and your college roommate floats down from the overstuffed shelf. You haven't seen this person in years and wonder what he is up to. Later that day, you hear the song you always used to listen to together while hanging out in your dorm room. That evening, your phone rings. Before you even answer, you know it's going to be your old roommate. And it is—he's calling to share some significant information about his life. Did the picture falling down from your bookcase or the song playing on the radio have anything to do with this forgotten person's sudden reappearance in your life? Or was it all just a crazy coincidence? Jung would say that the interconnectedness of these events was a classic case of synchronicity. A higher consciousness knew that your roommate would be reconnecting with you that day, and you were given several signs to help you prepare. An even deeper experience of synchronicity would be dreaming of the roommate the night before and then getting the phone call, evidence that your subconscious was picking up on conscious events.

Cultural Context: In 1983 the Police released *Synchronicity*, their most famous album to date. The album featured not only the two title tracks but also "Every Breath You Take," "King of Pain," and "Wrapped Around Your Finger," three of the group's most enduring songs. The album's cover features Sting reading Jung's book, and the lyrics of "Synchronicity I" and "Synchronicity II" exhibit a true understanding of the complex theory.

63. **TALISMAN**

Other Names: Amulet; charm.

General Description: *A small object carried or worn to bring about good luck and/or protect against evil.* Talismans come in a nearly endless variety of forms—stones, carved replicas of animals, miniature gods or revered objects, letters, religious symbols, gems, phrases, charms, and so forth. They are generally worn as jewelry (most commonly on necklaces or bracelets) or carried in a pocket, though they may also be displayed in a home or business, used for medicinal cures, or employed in times of crisis.

Origins: The word *talisman* comes from the Arabic *tilasm*, meaning "to consecrate," which in turn comes from the Greek *talein*, "to consecrate," and *talesma*, "consecration ceremony." The concept of an object with magical powers dates back to times unrecorded by history. Every culture worldwide has specific symbolic objects, names, words, and images.

In Practice: To ensure that good luck follows wherever you go, and if you are convinced that averting the evil eye is advantageous as well, load up on lucky talismans. Stockpile elephants, ladybugs, scarabs, and rabbits' feet in your home, stuff them into your pockets, and hang them from chains around your neck or wrist. Affix a mezuzah to your doorpost and put a money cat in the window, next to a Laughing Buddha. Wear a red string with a hamsa on your left wrist and tie an evil-eye bead to your baby's stroller. Carry a lucky penny and a rosary, along with a clove of garlic, all of which you can use if you happen to come across any vampires. Once you feel sure you have covered all the bases, go about your day confidently. You are secure.

Cultural Context:

In 1983 Games Workshop produced a board game called "Talisman: The Magical Quest Game," developed by Robert Harris. Similar to the popular Dungeons and Dragons fantasy game, Talisman presented gamers with set characters who encountered various difficulties along their path to fulfilling the quest at the center of the board. Each character relies on a special magical talisman to aid in the adventure. Although currently out of print, current owners enjoy the game in the United States, England, Australia, Israel, Poland, and several other countries.

Related Superstitions:

Amber, Chai, Charm Bracelet, Cross, Elephant, Evil Eye Bead, Four-Leaf Clover, Hamsa, Horseshoe, Jade, Ladybug, Laughing Buddha, Locket, Lucky Penny, Maneki Neko, Mezuzah, Rabbit's Foot, Red String, Scarab

64.   **TAROT CARDS**

General
Description:

A deck of seventy-eight illustrated cards used for divination and self-interpretation.

Origins:

Tarot cards first appeared in the fifteenth century in Italy; they were invented as a game called Triumphs (Tarocchi), which is similar to bridge. Over time, the illustrated cards took on mystical connotations, and soon each was given specific characteristics and symbolism that turned the deck into something more profound. The cards spread throughout Europe and beyond and have been reinterpreted and tailored to various cultures, faiths, and preferences. Some of the major offshoots of the original tarot are the Marseilles, Rider-Waite-Smith, and Thoth decks. Today, there are feminist tarot cards, Kabbalah-inspired decks, and cards related to sports, professions, and sciences.

In Practice:

The art of reading tarot cards is highly developed and varies widely among many different cultural groups. One constant, however, is that the reader must be highly knowledgeable about tarot interpretation and the patterns in which the cards can appear, so it is best to visit an experienced reader.

At a Tarot reading, the seeker is asked to shuffle the cards and cut the deck. From that deck, the reader lays out a certain number of cards in a distinct pattern called a spread. The spread varies by reader and can be tailored to a particular seeker's needs. The number of cards depends on the type of spread. A horoscope spread, for example, uses twelve cards, one for each astrological sign, that are arranged in a circle around a thirteenth card, which represents the seeker. Each of the twelve cards represents the different aspects of personality determined by the sign. Other popular spreads include the Celtic cross, the tree of life, the birthday, and the dream interpretation.

Tarot cards are divided into two categories: major arcana and minor arcana. The word *arcana* is the plural of *arcanum*, which means "profound secret," referring to the mysteries of the universe and of nature. Thus the cards represent the inner workings of our lives and the world around us—our psyche, relationships, and surroundings.

The major arcana consists of twenty-two cards (twenty-one trump cards and one joker called "The Fool"). Each card represents a universal theme that can be applied to life. They feature specific symbolic imagery, and the chart opposite notes possible interpretations associated with each card. (Note: These are generalizations only; interpretations are highly subjective, based on the individual's experiences and the card reader's methods.)

Card	Value	Possible Interpretations
The Fool	0	New beginnings, spontaneity, inexperience
The Magician	I	Concentration, dexterity, manipulation
The High Priestess	II	Mystery, wisdom, instinct
The Empress	III	Love, sexuality, satisfaction
The Emperor	IV	Control, power, bravery
The Pope	V	Belief system, morals/values, tradition
The Lovers	VI	Passion/desire, union, intimacy
The Chariot	VII	Confrontation, willpower, anxiety
Strength	VIII	Stability, courage, discipline
The Hermit	IX	Solitude, isolation, reflection
The Wheel of Fortune	X	Cycles, sudden events, turning point
Justice	XI	Ethics, impartiality, major decision
The Hanged Man	XII	Abandonment, passivity, suspension
Death	XIII	Conclusion, loss, transition/transformation
Temperance	XIV	Moderation, healing, recovery
The Devil	XV	Lust, responsibility, discipline
The Tower	XVI	Ruin, chaos, revelation, danger
The Star	XVII	Hope, optimism, tranquility
The Moon	XVIII	Confusion, worry, nurturing
The Sun	XIX	Happiness, health, optimism
Judgment	XX	Redemption, forgiveness, rebirth
The World	XXI	Wholeness, harmony, completion

The minor arcana, consisting of fifty-six cards, is divided into four suits, each of which has ten number cards (the ace is 1, plus 2 through 10) and four face cards (page, knight, queen, king). This arcana represents the practical application of the universal themes found in the major arcana as manifested in our daily lives. The four suits correspond to the four elements, and each has distinct symbolism: The Staff (also called the Wand or Baton) suit represents the element of fire, our energy and creativity; the Cup represents water, our emotional and spiritual life; the Sword represents air, our intellectual life and ego; and the Coin represents earth, our material concerns and physical being.

Once the cards have been laid out according to a spread, the reader begins to interpret the specific grouping's meaning. Each location in the spread holds specific significance. There are placeholders for the past, present, and future as well as love, marriage, and death. Based on which card falls on what spot, a reader will be able to tell you what is happening (or about to happen) in your life.

Cultural Context:

In the 2006 Lindsay Lohan movie *Just My Luck*, the absurdly fortunate Ashley Albright is told by a tarot card reader (played by Tovah Feldshuh) that her fate will soon be switched with that of another person. Soon after, Ashley kisses a handsome stranger, sparks fly, the heel breaks off her shoe, she rips her dress, and she is arrested. Meanwhile, the handsome stranger,

until then an absurdly unlucky person, saves the life
of a music producer, who in turn rewards him with a
recording contract and a free luxury apartment.
Clearly, the reader had it right—apparently, all these
changes were "in the cards."

Related
Superstitions:

Fortune-Teller, I Ching, Psychic, Runes

"THIRD TIME'S A CHARM"

General
Description:
☺

*A catchphrase implying that if you fail to achieve a goal
the first two times, you are bound to strike gold on
attempt number three.* The saying is also used as a
charm invoked before the third attempt at accomplishing a goal.

Origins:

According to the Web site Phrase Finder (www.phras-
es.org.uk), the first known printed reference to this
phrase dates from 1839, when it appeared in
Elizabeth Barrett Browning's *Letters Addressed to R. H.
Horne*: "'The luck of the third adventure' is prover-
bial." Since Browning refers to the phrase's common
origins, clearly it had been in use long before her
nineteenth-century mention. However, the exact origins are unclear. Some theorists link the number 3
with luck because of the trinity. Others tie it to a
British legal case in which a man slated for death by

hanging was freed after he managed to escape execution three times.

Variations:

"If at first you don't succeed, try, try again!" and "Better luck next time!" are two English alternatives. In Israel, when you see a person for the third time in a seemingly random, coincidental way, it is common to say *Pa'am shlishit glida!* ("Third time, ice cream!"). In this tradition, you agree to get together for ice cream after that third meeting since obviously the forces of nature have been trying to convey your need to converse with each other. What about "Three Strikes and You're Out"? Although this rule belongs to the realm of baseball, as a catchphrase it is now commonly used to refer to quotidian matters. The underlying meaning is that if a person is unable to succeed despite "third time's a charm," the cause is lost.

In Practice:

"Third time's a charm" is often applied to dating strategies. For example, if a girl went out on one date with a doctor and a second date with a lawyer, both of whom she preferred not to see again, she might look forward to her date with the trapeze artist in the hope that the third time will be the charm.

Cultural
Context:

The charm of the third time is featured prominently in William Shakespeare's *Merry Wives of Windsor*: "This is the third time; I hope good luck lies in odd numbers. . . . There is divinity in odd numbers, either in nativity, chance, or death."

Related
Superstitions:

"Bread and Butter," "Break a Leg," "God Bless You"

65.

UNICORN

General
Description:

A mythical creature typically depicted as a white horse-like animal with a single horn emanating from the head, a goat's beard, a lion's tail, and cloven hooves. The unicorn is a symbol of such varied virtues as virginity, chastity, fertility, and sexual attraction and is also thought to bring about general good luck and to offer protection from evil forces. Although no scientific evidence proves the existence of unicorns, they are popular worldwide and many people believe in them.

Origins:

From the Latin *uni* ("one") and *cornu* ("horn"), the unicorn remains mysterious and its history unclear. The King James Bible translates the Hebrew word *re'eim* (an animal that has no clear modern equivalent) as "unicorn," and the creature is mentioned in writings in Indian culture as well. A medieval folktale about a wild unicorn being miraculously tamed when it laid down and fell asleep in the lap of a virgin (often depicted as the Virgin Mary) led to its association with female virgins and Christianity.

Variations:	The Chinese unicorn, called Kilin, looks nothing like the Western notion of the beautiful animal. The Kilin is also considered to be a symbol of good luck and the harbinger of good fortune (for example, a Kilin predicted the birth of Confucius to his pregnant mother in 551 BCE). The Kilin is also depicted as a gentle creature that eats only plant matter that has already been severed from the earth. With the body of a deer, the tail of an ox, the hooves of a horse, and a short, single horn, the multicolored creature is revered as one of the four luckiest animals in Chinese mythology (along with the phoenix, dragon, and tortoise).
In Practice:	Before searching for a way to find a unicorn, you should first come to terms with the fact that the animal does not exist, even though some fan clubs insist to the contrary. You have about as much chance of encountering a unicorn prancing through the woods as of discovering the Loch Ness monster swimming in a Scottish lake. However, if you still want to try, the best strategy is to send a young, virginal girl into a quiet forest. If her intentions are pure, she will attract a unicorn, which will place its head in her lap and fall asleep. Once that occurs, the sleeping animal is yours for the taking.
Cultural Context:	The unicorn has been used throughout the ages as a symbol in literature, music, and politics; one is even featured on the royal arms of Scotland and the United

Kingdom. Especially prominent in fantasy literature, these mystical creatures have appeared in the works of William Shakespeare (*Julius Ceasar*, *The Tempest*), Lewis Carroll (*Through the Looking Glass*), and Tennessee Williams (*The Glass Menagerie*). A classic twentieth-century depiction of the unicorn appears in Ridley Scott's landmark 1985 sci-fi film *Legend*, starring Tom Cruise and Mia Sara. When the Lord of Darkness kidnaps Princess Lily and the last living unicorn, threatening to eliminate daylight forever by marrying the fairy girl and killing the unicorn, a forest boy named Jack must find a way to save the day.

66. **UNLUCKY NUMBER 13**

General Description:

The digit that comes between 12 and 14. The number 13 is particularly unfortunate in Western culture.

Origins:

Systems of numerology have been a part of nearly every culture for millennia. Examples include the Jewish Kabbalistic system of gematria, the Hindu Vedas, and Chinese numerology, thus proving that humans have long searched for the deeper meaning of mathematics and of numbers themselves. In the West, 13 is the most infamous unlucky number. One explanation for its bad-luck associations can be found in the Christian religion. The Last Supper was attended by thirteen guests—Jesus and his twelve apostles, with

Judas Iscariot, the traitor, as the thirteenth (see "In Practice"). In addition, Christ's crucifixion is believed to have taken place on Friday the thirteenth.

In Practice: Whatever you do, avoid being the thirteenth and final guest to arrive at a dinner party. If, as a host, you must set the table for thirteen, everyone should be seated and rise to leave the table simultaneously, since superstition holds that the first to stand or the last to sit is fated to die. This notion is related to the Last Supper: During that fateful meal, Jesus was the first to rise after the Last Supper and was later killed, and Judas was the last to be seated and took his own life just after Christ's crucifixion.

Cultural Context: Many office buildings choose to "skip" the thirteenth floor, as you may notice on the elevator when the buttons jump from 12 to 14. In addition, rooms may be numbered 12, 12A, 14 to fool the superstitious.

Related Superstitions: Chai, Friday the Thirteenth, Lucky Number 7

VEDIC ASTROLOGY

General Description: *The Indian version of astrology and horoscope readings used to predict success and failure in relationships, career, personal choices, and life in general.* Indian astrologers have different names for each of the twelve zodiac signs of the Western horoscope. Aries is Mesha, Taurus is Vrishabha, Gemini is Mithuna, Cancer is Karkata, Leo is Simha, Virgo is Kanya, Libra is Tula, Scorpio is Vrishchika, Sagittarius is Dhanu, Capricorn is Makar, Aquarius is Kumbha, and Pisces is Meena.

The basic structure of the two systems is similar. However, unlike Western astrology, the Vedic system assumes that the stars are the fixed points around which the movements of the planets are measured. In addition, the Western zodiac follows a tropical chart (based on the sun), whereas the Vedic system follows the sidereal zodiac (based on the moon). As a result, an Aries according to the Western tropical zodiac is a Pisces in the Vedic sidereal zodiac.

Origins: Also known as Jyotish, from the Sanskrit words *jyot* ("light") and *isha* ("lord"), Vedic astrology is the study of how divinity manifests itself in the realms of space and time. It dates to about 1500 BCE.

In Practice: Beyond reading into your personality tendencies and determining how your sign will relate and interact with other signs, Vedic astrologers may suggest various stones and gems, mantras and yantras, or herbs and rituals to aid in balancing your energies and resolving issues. They also focus on your karma—the residue of your past lives as manifested in this incarnation—and how that karma helps you understand experiences in your current life.

The Vedic signs, called *rashis*, correspond to the twelve signs familiar to followers of Western astrology. However, because they are determined by the placement of the moon, each sign has different dates every year. Vedic astrologers must consult a heavy tome called an ephemeris, which charts the positions of the planets at any point throughout the ages. Therefore, be sure to tell your astrologer the year of your birth as well as the day of the month to determine your exact sign.

Cultural Context:

Many Indians are especially enamored of two things: Bollywood movies and Vedic astrology. They may spend hours analyzing the likelihood of various occurrences, consulting the stars about the fate of their children with the help of the myriad twenty-four-hour-a-day astrology channels available in the country. Not surprisingly, when Aishwarya Rai, a famous Bollywood actress and former Miss World, became engaged in 2007 to fellow actor Abhishek Bachchan, their Vedic match was the focus of popular attention. Alas, Rai is a *manglik*, a person whose birth position in Mars portends an untimely death or serious illness for his or her spouse. To avoid passing on this curse to Bachchan, Rai's family made sure that she married someone else—or, rather *something* else. A banana tree stood in for Bachchan at a symbolic ceremony before the couple's official wedding, effectively transferring the bad luck to the plant.

Related
Superstitions: Astrological Horoscope, Karma, Mantra, Talisman,
Yantra

67.   **VOODOO DOLLS**

Other Name: Wanga dolls.

General
Description: *Small, stick-figure dolls, often stuffed with hay, that are*
used to place curses and spells on one's enemies or to con-
jure positive experiences. Although the dolls are more
popularly known for their role in evil-doing, they can
also be called upon to aid with healing or to bring
good luck.

Origins: The voodoo doll is a modern offshoot of the ancient
traditions of the voodoo (or vodun) religion of West
Africa, a tradition that is thousands of years old.
Voodoo was brought to Haiti via slaves forcibly taken
from West African countries. That is also how voodoo
reached the southern United States, where it is most
prominent in the Bayou region, especially in New
Orleans. The Afro-Caribbean faith is still dominant in
Haiti and New Orleans; it has been the official religion of Benin, Africa, since 1996.

The voodoo doll is in fact not an official part of
the voodoo religion. Rather, it stems from the tradition of black magic known as hoodoo, which his
often mistaken for the more widespread voodoo.

Although voodoo incorporates many rituals, it does not include black magic.

Variations: In true voodoo rituals, followers beat drums, shake rattles, and dance among lit candles and effigies until someone, usually a priest or priestess, reaches a trance-like state of ecstasy, during which a spirit overtakes the body. Once filled with the divine spirit, the priest/priestess is thought to have temporary supernatural powers. This ritual is meant to be used for good, not evil.

In Practice: Voodoo dolls are most often used to place a curse on an enemy by sticking pins into an effigy, placing the prickly points in locations where one would like to inflict pain on the victim. Yet, the dolls are supposed to be made with healing energies in mind and were originally intended to be used for the good of humanity. When a doll becomes cursed with the negative energy of someone seeking vengeance, it can no longer be used for positive purposes. In that case, it should then be sprinkled with holy water and set ablaze. It must then be wrapped in a white cloth and buried far away from the home; furthermore, this deed should be done on a Saturday. The earth will recycle its negative energies and replace them with blessing.

Cultural Context: Voodoo and wanga dolls are commonly available via the Internet. Different types aid with love, money, career, sex, friendship, weight loss, gambling, and luck, to name just a few popular causes. Hex dolls are also available. In 2006 hex dolls became so popular in China that worried government officials banned their sale to the public.

Related
Superstitions:

Akuaba

68.

WALKING UNDER A LADDER

General
Description:

🙁

The act of passing below an extended ladder, usually one leaning against a wall or building facade. Doing so brings bad luck.

Origins:

☠ ✝

There are several theories behind the tradition of avoiding ladders. One contends that in the days before gallows, men were hung on the top rung of a ladder, and their spirits were thought to linger underneath. After the invention of the gallows, the condemned often had to walk under the platform and through the legs of the ladder before ascending to the gibbet. Both associations are equally gloomy. In a more spiritual vein, an open ladder, or one that is leaning against a building for support, forms a triangle, a shape associated with the Holy Trinity. Some Christians believe that disrupting the Trinity by walking through it (or its symbol) was tantamount to provoking the Devil himself.

In Practice: Fortunately, there are ways to undo the damage of
                 walking under a ladder. First double back around the
                 ladder and go under it again, this time walking back-
                 ward. You might also choose to spit three times
                 through the ladder's rungs, or once on your shoe,
                 before continuing along your path. Just to be on the
                 safe side, cross your fingers and keep them crossed
                 until you see a dog. If you perform these actions, the
                 curse placed upon you will be reversed and you will
                 once again be safe.

                     Although many people agree that it's best to avoid
                 walking under a ladder, few stop to think that this
                 piece of advice is practical as well. What if something
                 falls on you? What if, while walking under the device,
                 you bump into it, causing it to fall and injure either
                 the person on it or someone standing below? These
                 are all good reasons to steer clear of an open ladder.

Cultural   Ladders have long been laden with profound symbol-
Context: ism. The best known is the biblical reference to
                 Jacob's Ladder, which extends from the heavens to
                 earth and serves as the device on which angels ascend
                 and descend. Swiss psychiatrist Carl Jung believed
                 that the symbol of a ladder, and specifically its
                 appearance in dreams, signified the collective uncon-
                 scious desire for spiritual growth and the experience
                 of individuation. Fellow analyst Sigmund Freud
                 argued that dreaming of a ladder (or, more commonly,
                 climbing a flight of stairs) was yet another reference

to sexual intercourse: Climbing a ladder or staircase involves a rhythmical pattern of motion, and by the time you reach the top, you are out of breath. One wonders how Jung and Freud may have interpreted a dream about walking under a ladder—perhaps as the desire to erase self-knowledge or to avoid sex? Just a guess.

Related Superstitions: Fingers Crossed, Spitting

69. **WISHBONE**

General Description: *The furcula bone (fused collar bones) of a bird, usually a chicken or turkey, that is shaped like the letter Y.*

Origins: As long ago as 400 BCE, the Etruscans believed that roosters and hens possessed prophetic powers, mainly because the animals cackle before laying eggs and crow before dawn. Since hens were considered powerful creatures, the Etruscans would test their prophetic abilities by placing one in the middle of a circle divided into twenty sections, each representing a letter of their alphabet. As the hen pecked her way through the grain spread across the circle, the Etruscans believed she was spelling out a message of great import. The hen was then sacrificed, and the wishbone was saved as a lucky symbol. People would touch the bone in the hope that it would grant their wishes.

The Romans put a distinctively competitive stamp on the tradition, declaring that the bone should be broken by two people and that whoever came away with the larger half would be the one whose wish would be granted. The Roman custom eventually made its way into British tradition. When the British began settling North America, they found the best wishbone of all in the native American turkey, hence the widespread Thanksgiving tradition.

In Practice: Two people take hold of either end of the wishbone and pull to break it; whoever is left with the larger section will be granted a wish. If you are particularly fond of the wish-granting power of the poultry clavicle but don't feel like roasting turkeys to get one, consider buying a charm or amulet to wear on a bracelet or key chain. Though these representations usually show unbroken bones, they are rife with wishing potential.

Cultural Context: These days, wishbones are less popular, especially among vegetarians and animal rights activists. Like the rabbit's foot, synthetic versions are now available, so you can make your wish without running afoul of any turkeys. Also available is the "Lucky Break Wishbone," made entirely of recyclable plastic and sold in groups of four or five, which means no more fighting over who gets to break the wishbone.

Related
Superstitions:

Charm Bracelet, Rabbit's Foot

70. **WISHING WELL**

General
Description:
☺

A naturally occurring or human-made structure for extracting water from underground aquifers that, according to folkloric tradition, is capable of granting wishes. Most common is to throw a penny into the well to have your wish granted and receive good luck.

Origins:

As far back as the fourteenth century, Europeans made pilgrimages to significant holy wells—those that had been blessed by saints or ascribed healing properties. The religious pilgrims believed that the wells housed spiritual powers, so throwing a coin or other possession into one was akin to a sacrificial act, and in return the wish would be granted. Water has always been acknowledged as a source of life. Thus, wells, lakes, and other bodies of water have held special significance, especially for land-locked communities.

Variations:

At one time, many people had wells on their property from which they drew all the water necessary for their daily lives. Today, most communities are equipped with complex waterworks systems, making the backyard well obsolete. Yet a wish-granting water source is usually only as far your local mall. Shopping-center fountains are often littered with coins tossed by those hoping that their luck will improve or that their wishes will be granted.

In Practice: When you come across a well (or other water source, such as a fountain in an urban area or a waterfall in the jungle), you must first believe in the water's power to grant your wish. Next, make your wish—silently, for it will only be granted if you do not tell anyone what it is. Then throw in your penny and wait for your luck to improve. (Note: Some believe that you should make the wish only when you hear the penny hit the water, but that may be difficult to discern.)

Cultural   The luckiest wishing well in the world is in Tuuri,
Context: Finland. The word *tuuri* means "luck" in Finnish, and the small southern village of five hundred has become a major tourist attraction. Legend has it that Lady Luck calls Tuuri her home, and she lives there with her lucky white unicorn that occasionally drops his gold horseshoe that is attached with seven diamond pins. The village boasts a giant wishing well that is guaranteed to grant the wish you hope for, as long as (a) you truly believe in the power of the well, and (b) you wish for something to happen to a friend, not for yourself.

Related
Superstitions: Lucky Penny

YANTRA

General
Description: *A drawing of intricate geometric, interlocking patterns*
                used in Indian culture as a visual tool for meditation.
ॐ   From the Sanskrit words *yam* ("to support") and *trana*
                ("freedom"), a yantra is a "loom," as in a way of weav-
                ing your own consciousness. Yantras are drawn to rep-
                resent Hindu gods and their energies, astrological
                signs, significant numbers, and personal qualities.
                They are often symmetrical and have a focal point
                that draws the eye to the center. By meditating on a
                yantra, one hopes to manifest the energies represented
                by the patterns, suppress evil forces, or control the
                mind to bring about positive experiences.

Origins: In ancient times, yantras were used as visual diagrams
                of verbal mantras and regarded as the manifestation of
                the energies of venerable gods and goddesses.

Variations: Each yantra has a particular mantra with which it is
                associated. A mantra is a word, phrase, or syllable that
                is repeated, either orally or silently, to achieve a state
                of heightened awareness and spiritual power. (See
                page 151.)

In Practice: Specific yantras already exist, the most famous being the Sri Yantra, composed of nine interlocking triangles surrounding a central dot known as a *bindu*. Yantras may also be reinvented or re-created for personalization. You can choose to create one using lines, geometrical shapes, and figures that are based on a birth date, a planet, a revered god or goddess, or a virtue you hope to possess. Constructing your personal yantra may continue throughout your lifetime since your goals and worldview will inevitably change as you grow and develop spiritually.

Cultural   One branch of Indian spiritual practice that makes
Context: creative use of the yantra is Tantric yoga and meditation. Americans are most familiar with Tantra in the form of Tantric sex, a popular area of spiritual practice. Tantric sex is based on the idea that enlightenment can be reached through our physical bodies. By achieving the deepest union of male and female partners, we help unite the disparate forces of the universe and return to the ultimate center of existence, the awareness of our true selves and the truths of the universe. In an elaborate system of extended foreplay and exercises encouraging multiple orgasms in both partners, Tantric sex elevates sexual ecstasy to cosmic proportions.

Tantra is based on the belief that the universe was created from the splitting of a single, unifying point of energy. From that initial point, male and female energies divided, repeatedly multiplying until the complex world as we know it was formed. Humans are miniature versions of the universe, beginning as tiny cells and becoming more complex as they grow. On a spiritual level, we are composed of opposing forces, and our ultimate goal is to unite the divided energies within us and reach our center. This pattern of expansion from a central place is the basic concept of a yantra, so it is natural that the yantra—which is essentially a diagram that develops from a central focus—is used in visual Tantric meditation.

Related   Mantra
Superstitions:

Sources

BOOKS AND ARTICLES

Bergen, Fanny D. "Some Saliva Charms," in *The Journal of American Folklore* 3, no. 8 (Jan–Mar 1890), pp. 51–59.

D'Souza, Barbara. "Why Fat Jokes Aren't Funny," accessed at http://www.usatoday.com (accessed 4/29/07).

Dobson, Roger. "How the Moon Rules Your Life," in *The Independent*, 21 (January 2007).

Fontana, David. *The Secret Language of Symbols: A Visual Key to Symbols and Their Meanings.* San Francisco: Chronicle Books, 1993.

Hoffman, Beth. "Wishbone Lined to Luck and History," *Cape Cod Times*, November 23, 2005.

Lumsden, Michael, "Cow Care Change in India," *Christian Science Monitor*, Date TK.

Pattanaik, Devdutt. *Lakshmi: The Goddess of Wealth and Fortune—An Introduction.* Mumbai: Vakils Feffer & Simons, Ltd., 2003.

Place, Robert M. *The Tarot: History, Symbolism, and Divination.* New York: Tarcher, Penguin, 2005.

Pogrebin, Robin. "It Seems the Cards Do Lie: A Police Sting Cracks Down on Fortune-Telling Fraud," *New York Times*, June 30, 1999.

Reid, Lori. *The Art of Hand Reading*. New York: DK Publishing, Inc., 1996.

Shmerling, Dr. Robert H., M. D. "Toads and Frogs—Friends or Foes?" at http://www.intelihealth.com (accessed 3/5/07)

Somerville, Neil. *Your Chinese Horoscope 2005*. London: Element, 2004.

VanArsdale, Daniel W. "Chain Letter Evolution," accessed at http://www.silcom.com (accessed 1/21/07).

Vyse, Styart A. *Believing in Magic: The Psychology of Superstition*. New York: Oxford University Press, 1997.

Waring, Philippa. *Dictionary of Omens and Superstitions*. New Jersey: Chartwell Books, Inc., 1986.

Wiseman, Richard. *The Luck Factor: Changing Your Luck, Changing Your Life*. New York: Hyperion, 2003.

WEB SITES

http://buddhism.kalachakranet.org

http://chinese.astrology.com

http://hinduism.about.com/library

http://law.onecle.com/new-york/penal/PEN0165.35_165.35.html

http://www.africancraftsmarket.com/dollsakuaba_details.htm

http://www.astrology-numerology.com

http://www.en.wikipedia.org

http://www.ethnographica.com/pages/Asante9.php?project_id=9

http://www.exoticindiaart.com/article/symbols

http://www.fourleafclover.com/4fact.html

http://www.goodluckboutique.com/

http://www.horoscopes.com

http://www.learntarot.com

http://www.luckymojo.com/horseshoe.html

http://www.museumoftalkingboards.com/index.html

http://www.mymotherscharms.com/history.htm

http://www.nativetech.org/dreamcat/dreamcat.html

http://www.oldsuperstitions.com

http://www.phrases.org.uk

http://www.powerfortunes.com/luckycharms.html

http://www.sanatansociety.org/yoga_and_meditation/yantra_meditation.htm

http://www.scottishwhiteheather.com/heatherstory.html

http://www.snopes.com/luck/cookie.asp

http://www.snopes.com/luck/luck.asp

http://www.thefoolsday.com/

http://www.thingsasian.com/stories-photos/1725

http://www.worldwidewords.org/qa/qa-bre1.htm

http://www.dnaindia.com/report.asp?NewsID=1091918
http://www.theforbiddenknowledge.com/wtc/index02.htm
http://www.usmint.gov/about_the_mint/fun_facts/index.cfm?flash=yes&a
ction=fun_facts2a

Glossary

Angida. This monk, who attained *bodhi* due to his kindness, is usually depicted laughing and carrying a sack. According to legend, he was a talented snake catcher who trapped venomous snakes in his handy bag, removed their fangs, and released them so that they wouldn't hurt anyone. His name also means "calico bag."

Arcanum. Usually plural, arcana. Profound secrets; mysterious, specialized knowledge possessed only by the initiated.

Arjuna. This warrior and master archer is a central figure in Hindu mythology, and he is one of the main semidivine heroes in the Hindu epic *Mahabharata*. His name means "bright," "shining," and "silver." Lord Krishna revealed the *Bhagavad Gita* to Prince Arjuna; the text of this holy book is a record of their conversation. Their relationship represents an ideal for all humankind: a mortal guided by god.

Artemis. In Greek mythology, the goddess of the hunt and the wild. She is also goddess of the moon, and her twin brother, Apollo, is god of the sun.

Artha. This Sanskrit term can mean "cause," "meaning," "motive," "notion," and "purpose." It also connotes material prosperity and wealth. In Hinduism, it is one of the four goals of life (called *purusharthas*) and is above kama but below dharma and moksha.

Ashtamangala. Sanskrit for the eight auspicious objects (or signs); see page 70. These lucky signs are endemic to many cultures and are especially important in Buddhist symbolism. They are used as teaching tools to illuminate qualities of mind and consciousness.

Atum. This hermaphroditic deity in Egyptian mythology is known as "the complete one" and as a creator and finisher of the world. His name may have been derived from the word *tem*, which means "to finish."

bagua. This ancient Chinese diagram is a fundamental philosophical concept. It is usually octagonal with a trigram on each side; sections correspond to different aspects of our lives. The concepts the bagua map embodies apply not only to Taoist thought and the I Ching, but also to feng shui, martial arts, and even navigation.

bashert. Yiddish for "destiny," this term has romantic connotations; it is often used to refer to one's heavenly preordained soul mate.

Bast. This ancient Egyptian goddess's name means "(female) devourer." She was first depicted as a woman with a lion's head. As Egyptian cats became important companions and devourers of vermin such as rats and cobras—often eating from their owner's plates and wearing gold jewelry—Bast became the protector of smaller felines. She was then depicted as a domestic cat deity. More than 300,000 mummified cats were discovered when her temple at Per-Bast was excavated.

Bhagavad Gita. Sanskrit for "song of God," this text is a selection from the epic *Mahabharata*. Lord Krishna reveals the *Bhagavad Gita* to Arjuna, explaining dharma, the idea of duty and universal harmony. Krishna describes that he incarnates each era to establish righteousness and harmony in the world.

bilva fruit. Also known as the wood apple, the bilva fruit is one of the eight auspicious symbols of Buddhism. It looks like a large, reddish brown apple and signifies livelihood and right action (which bears good fruit) in the eight-fold path.

bodhi. A Sanskrit word for the enlightenment and awakened consciousness of a fully liberated yogi. It indicates a complete and perfect sanity and awareness of the universe. As a bodhi, one is freed from the indefinitely repeating cycle of samsara (birth, suffering, death, and rebirth).

Brahma. This Hindu god of creation is one of the trimurti (along with Vishnu, the preserver, and Shiva, the destroyer) and consort of the goddess Saraswati, the goddess of learning. His name is also the nominative singular of brahman, which means super-soul, spiritual source of the universe, and supreme omnipresent existence of all things.

chirognomy. Foretelling the future by studying the lines and markings on the palm; this is a category of palmistry. Also called chiromancy.

dermatoglyphics. The scientific study of fingerprints and a category of palmistry. Dermatoglyphs are a window into a critical period of a person's embryogenesis; atypical dermatoglyphs may be related to genetic disorders.

dharma. This Sanskrit term is a concept of universal harmony and duty. In Hinduism, it is one of the four goals of life (called purusharthas); these are also the four arms of the goddess Lakshmi. Dharma is above kama and artha but below moksha. It is revealed to Arjuna by Lord Krishna in the *Bhagavad Gita*.

dharmachakra. One of the eight auspicious symbols of Buddhism, this wheel of doctrine (or wheel of law) symbolizes dharma (law) in Hinduism.

Diwali. A major Indian festival at the end of the Hindu month of Ashwayuja (in October/November) that celebrates the triumph of good over evil. During this "festival of lights," lanterns, lamps, and fireworks are lit to celebrate hope for humankind.

Dodecatheon. This genus of herbaceous, flowering plant has basal clumps of leaves and nodding, starlike flowers. The flowers droop from long thin stalks, and the petals are bent back, creating the effect of a shooting star.

doxology. A hymn or liturgical expression praising God.

Druids. Ancient class of priests, scholars, magistrates, and healers. The Celtic word *Druid* means "finding/knowing the oak tree" and connotes steadfastness. Much of what we know about the Druids comes from Julius Caesar's records; Druids were supplanted by the Roman government and, later, by Christianity. In Ireland, Druidic practices continued even as Christianity took hold. Scholars opine that the Western Celtic Druid and Eastern Hindu Brahma are lateral survivals of an ancient Indo-European priesthood.

durva grass. An incredibly resilient grass that symbolizes long life. In Buddhism, it is believed to be immortal, and thus it overcomes samsara (the successive death and rebirth of all things).

ephemeris. A tabular statement of the assigned places of celestial bodies for regular intervals, used by Vedic astrologers to determine birth signs.

extrasensory perception (ESP). A paranormal ability to obtain information via extrasensory means; this term is used to describe psychic skills such as clairvoyance, telepathy, and precognition.

fu. A Chinese word for luck. Also a character of *Fu Lu Shou*, a term that means "good fortune," and an ancient Taoist theory of luck and good fortune that represents the three desires of ordinary people. These three—luck in wealth, rank, and longevity—are often personified and can be seen as gods of happiness, prosperity, and longevity throughout Chinese artwork.

furcula. A forked bone formed by the fusion of two clavicles; it is found in birds as well as theropod dinosaurs. In Latin, it means "little fork." Structurally, it strengthens the thoracic skeleton so that it can withstand flight. The furcula is commonly referred to as the wishbone; see page 215.

Ganesha. This elephant-headed Hindu deity is worshipped by a wide variety of sects. He is the god of beginnings and the god of obstacles, the god of intellect and wisdom, and a special patron of the arts and sciences. He is affectionately honored at the start of any ceremony, and he is invoked at the beginning of any text as the "Patron of Letters."

gaushala. A Sanskrit word meaning "house of cow," these are special cow reserves in rural areas outside city limits. Holy Indian city cows are often sent to these locales so that they will be protected and cared for (and so they'll no longer hold up city traffic).

gematria. A numerology of the Hebrew alphabet that is used to derive meaning from geometrical relationships. Hebrew gematria is the best known today, but Greek gematria predates it by centuries.

gibbet. Another term for the gallows, a guillotine, or any structure used for execution. Also used as a term for the structures built to publicly display executed corpses (or parts of corpses), an action that supposedly deters crime.

Gregorian calendar. The most widely used calendar in the world today. Pope Gregory XIII introduced this arithmetical, Christian calendar in 1582 as a revision of the Julian calendar. It was adopted in Great Britain and the American colonies in 1752.

hilaria. Ancient Roman festivals celebrated at the vernal equinox to honor Cybele, the deification of the fertile earth goddess.

holi. A Hindu and Sikh spring festival, also called the Dolyatra or the Festival of Colors. During the event, people playfully throw water and colored powders—made from ayurvedic medicinal herbs—at each other.

hoodoo. Traditional African folk magic brought to the southern United States from West and Central Africa by enslaved peoples. Hoodoo conjuring allows people to access their supernatural powers to improve their lives and imbues common items with magical powers, such as the mojo amulet. Not to be mistaken for voodoo.

hotei. The Japanese name for the Laughing Buddha. He is known as Pu-Tai in China and is one of the seven lucky gods.

ichthys. An ancient and classical Greek word for "fish." Among Christians, it has been used as a symbol for Jesus Christ since the end of the first century CE.

jadeite. A dense pyroxene mineral and one of the two minerals (the other is nephrite) recognized as the gemstone jade, which is imbued with good luck. It is formed in metamorphic rocks at a high pressure and low temperatures.

jinni. The Arabic term for a genie (also written *djinni*), a member of a race of supernatural creatures called the jinn (or *djinn*). "Jinn" literally means anything that connotes invisibility, seclusion, and remoteness.

Julian calendar. Introduced in Rome in 46 BCE, it established the 12-month year of 365 days, with 366 days in each fourth year and 31 or 30 days in the months.

kama. This Sanskrit term indicates sensual gratification, aesthetic enjoyment, love, and sexual fulfillment. In Hinduism, it is the first of the four goals of life (called purusharthas); these are also the four arms of the goddess Lakshmi. It is the first of these, below dharma, artha, and moksha.

Khepri. A minor god in ancient Egypt who is associated with the dung beetle, or scarab, as well as the cycle of life, death, and rebirth. Because dung beetles tirelessly roll balls of dung, ancient Egyptians came to regard them as a solar deity associated with the forces that ceaselessly move the sun across the sky.

Kilin. A chimerical, mythical Chinese creature, similar to the Western concept of a unicorn; this hoofed beast is said to appear when a sage arrives. Seeing one is a very good omen that brings *rui* (a combination of serenity and/or prosperity). A kilin may seem terrifying or appear to have flames all over its body, but it only punishes the wicked—and it is a vegetarian. It is generally a peaceful creature that can walk on grass without disturbing it. In recent centuries, it has come to look like a stylized image of a giraffe.

komboloi. A strand of Greek worry beads that resemble prayer beads such as rosaries but have no religious significance. They are used for relaxation, to manage stress, and to pass the time. Typically, they are made from an organic material that is pleasant to handle and feature an odd number of beads, a fixed bead at the head, and a tassle.

Krishna. A Hindu deity worshipped as an incarnation of Vishnu. Krishna usually appears as a young cowherd playing a flute or as a young prince giving philosophical guidance. He is often depicted as blue or black, as his name literally means "dark" in Sanskrit; in the Brahma Samhita his skin is described as being tinged with the hue of clouds.

Lakshmi. A Hindu goddess of light, wisdom, wealth, fortune, and the lotus flower. She is the consort of Narayan, the supreme being, and is believed to be the mother of the universe. She is loved for her motherly nature and is thought of as a patron of luck, beauty, courage, and fertility.

manglik. According to Vedic astrology, a person whose birth position on Mars portends an illness or untimely death for his or her spouse.

mendhi. The elaborate application of henna, typically done for special occasions and celebrations, especially weddings.

Moirae. The three fates in Greek mythology: Clotho, the spinner; Lachesis, the apportioner; and Atropos, the inevitable. These sisters control the destinies of all beings, mortal and immortal.

moksha. This Sanskrit term means liberation and release. In Hinduism, it is the ultimate goal of the four goals of life (called purusharthas); these are also the four arms of the goddess Lakshmi. Moksha is the highest of these, above kama, artha, and dharma.

nephrite. One of two minerals recognized as the gemstone jade (the other is jadeite), a gem known for its luck-attracting qualities.

numerology. A study of the occult significance of numbers. It can refer to any one of the many traditions, systems, and beliefs in an esoteric relationship between people (or objects) and numbers.

palmistry. An art of reading hands to determine a person's traits, talents, and future fate. It can be divided into several subcategories, such as chirognomy, chiromancy, and dermatoglyphics.

paraskevidekatria. Fear of Friday the thirteenth.

Parcae. This is the name of the three fates in Roman mythology. The Romans called them Nona, Decima, and Morta. These sisters control the destinies of all beings, mortal and immortal.

penni. A former monetary unit, equal to 1/100 Finnish markka. It was the smallest unit of the currency of Finland from 1860 until the euro's introduction in 2002. The word penni was derived from the Germanic pfennig.

pfennig. An old German coin that was used from the 9th century until the euro was introduced in 2002. Valuable in the Middle Ages, it lost value through the centuries. The last pfennigs made with traces of silver were minted in 1805 and are quite rare. The English penny, Polish fenig, and Finnish penni are etymologically related.

psychikos. This ancient Greek word means, literally, acts of charity. The related Greek word psuksos refers to the spirit, motive force, psyche, or soul; it can be used to describe the consciousness of an individual, or the animating principle of the world and universal consciousness. It is also the name of several towns in Greece.

Purim. Jewish holiday celebrated on the fourteenth of Adar (in March) commemorating the survival of the Jews. On the 13th of Adar in the fifth century BCE, Haman, royal vizier to the Persian king, plotted a massacre of all Jews. This festival celebrates their deliverance, and is told in the Old Testament Book of Esther.

purusharthas. The four goals of Hinduism; these are also the four arms of the goddess Lakshmi. In ascending order, they are kama, artha, dharma, and moksha.

Pu-Tai. The Chinese name for the Laughing Buddha. He is known as Hotei in Japan and is one of the seven lucky gods.

Ra. The Egyptian sun god and chief deity. Also written as "Re."

rishi. A Vedic sage and an inspired seer; one to whom the Vedic hymns have been revealed. Rishis memorize the Vedas in the language they regard as the most perfect, Sanskrit.

samsara. In many religions, the endless cycle of reincarnation: birth, suffering, death, and rebirth.

Shiva. A main deity of Hinduism. Within Shaivism, Shiva is the principal deity; in other branches of Hinduism, such as the Smarta tradition, he is worshipped as one of many manifestations of the divine. Within the *trimurti*, Shiva is the destroyer, the transformer.

Tarocchi. A game played with a Tarot deck of playing cards. The decks used for divination are typically ill-suited for playing because the corner symbols are missing.

Thor. A warrior deity common to all early Germanic peoples. His name is the early Germanic word for thunder. Thor's hammer, Mjollnir, represents lightning and has many supernatural powers; it is often carved on runic stones and funerary stelae.

trimurti. This Sanskrit word for "three forms" is, in Hinduism, a triad of the three great gods: Brahma (creation), Vishnu (maintenance), and Shiva (destruction). They are syncretic personalities, known through their many incarnations.

triskaidekaphobia. Fear of the number thirteen.

Tyche. The Greek word for "luck," Tyche is also the name of the Greek counterpart to the modern concept of Lady Luck. This goddess governed the fortune and prosperity of a city. She was often depicted carrying a cornucopia or the wheel of fate, and she appears on many Hellenistic coins.

voodoo. This West African spiritual system of faith and ritual practices was spread to North and South America, the Philippines, and the Caribbean by the African diaspora; it has been passed on through oral tradition, carrying genealogy, history, and fables to successive generations. It explains the forces of the universe and human nature and directs how to influence both. Adherents honor deities and venerate ancestors. Not to be confused with hoodoo.

Vishnu. A principle Hindu deity, member of the trimurti. He is the protector and preserver of the world; he maintains dharma (the moral order). Krishna is one of Vishnu's incarnations.

wo lou. In feng shui, this metal vase shaped like a gourd is placed in the center of a property to help bring blessings of health and longevity into the home.

yu. A Chinese word meaning "royal gem"; it is often used to refer to jade.

zodiac. An imaginary band in the heavens, centered on the ecliptic that encompasses the paths of the planets (excluding Pluto). It is divided into twelve constellations (the twelve signs). A zodiac can also be an image that represents the constellations of the zodiac and their symbols. More generally, a zodiac is a cyclic course.

Index

Numbers in **bold** (for example, **18**) can be used to locate illustrations of luck-related symbols and practices in the color-plate section. All other numbers are page numbers.

Acknowledgments

This book is first and foremost for my husband, Jeremy Wylen, who is my luckiest charm, my most enthusiastic cheerleader, and my best friend. Thank you for everything.

Thanks also go to Yablons and Wylens everywhere for their unfailing love and support. A girl couldn't ask for a nicer bunch of family members.

Finally, the stars must have been aligned when Mindy Brown of Quirk Books found me and suggested that I write this book, and then assigned the talented Kevin Kosbab and Mary Ellen Wilson to be my editors. Hats off to them and to the entire staff of Quirk Books.

More Quirk Field Guides

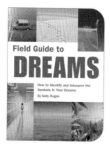

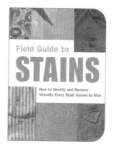